The Somerset and Dorset at Midford

MIDFORD – from the south-east: showing the S&D viaduct, signalbox and station, and, closer to the foreground, the GW Limpley Stoke-Camerton line. It is interesting to compare this undated picture (probably taken in the late 1940s and certainly pre-1953, when the station canopy was removed) with that on page 24.

On 1st September 1962 – the penultimate Saturday of through passenger traffic between the North of England, the Midlands and the south coast, via the S&D line – ex-S&D class 7F No. 53810, crosses Midford viaduct with the 10.40 am (SO) Exmouth-Cleethorpes train and enters the single-line section to Bath Junction. Midford viaduct carried the S&D over the remains of the Somersetshire Coal Canal, the Cam brook, and the GW branch line from Limpley Stoke to Camerton; the derelict and overgrown trackbed of which can be seen. Within a few years the S&D would suffer a similar fate.   B.J. Ashworth

The Somerset and Dorset
at
Midford

MIKE ARLETT

Millstream Books

Published 1986
Millstream Books
7 Orange Grove
Bath
Avon BA1 1LP

Text © M.J. Arlett 1986

Note: Ordnance Survey maps used in Chapters 1-3 are all
pre-1935, to the scale of 25 inches to 1 mile.
ISBN 0948975 024

Text set in 10/12 point Baskerville
Typeset by Kingfisher Railway Productions, 188 Bitterne
Road, Southampton.

Printed in Great Britain by Netherwood Dalton & Co.,
Bradley Mills, Huddersfield, Yorks.

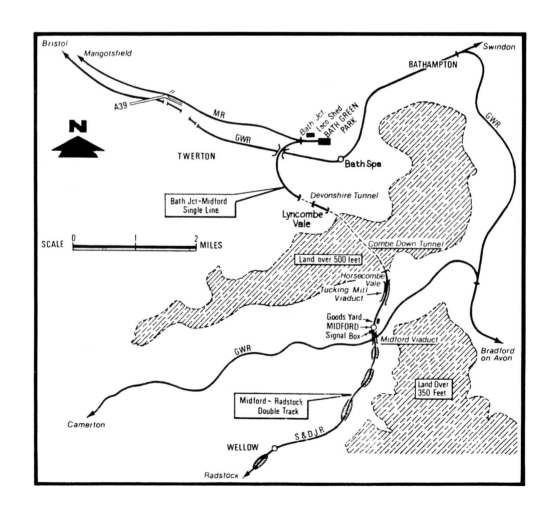

PREFACE

The genesis of this publication was a short book entitled *The Railways of Midford*, which I wrote for The Somerset & Dorset Railway Trust in 1983. Although well received, the limited format of that publication prevented me from incorporating a considerable amount of material about the Somerset & Dorset at Midford.

I was delighted therefore, when invited by Millstream Books, to prepare a revised and much enlarged edition, for this has provided the opportunity, not only to enhance my original text, but to include maps, diagrams and photographs etc., all of which were previously limited in number, or omitted through lack of space. To those who have read *The Railways of Midford* I apologise in advance for the inevitable repetition, but at least I have the opportunity to correct my previous errors of fact – whilst hopefully not introducing too many new ones! And in the knowledge that perhaps it is the pictorial content which sometimes influences the purchase of a railway book, I can with some certainty confirm that the majority of the photographs in this book are previously unpublished, at least within the format of a book.

The aim of this book has been not only to consolidate, from many separate sources, information already available about the S&D at Midford but to have added details and items of interest which may not have been previously published. Despite more than 25 years of research, some uncertainties still remain. Similarly, years of enquiries have failed to reveal any photographs of the construction of the line at or near Midford.

One point which, at this early stage, must be repeated from *The Railways of Midford* is the fact that, in relating the history of the S&D line, reference will of necessity be made to the 'other' railway that ran through Midford, the Great Western branch line from Limpley Stoke to Camerton. But, at Midford at least, for many years, it was the 'Serene and Delightful' – rather than 'God's Wonderful Railway' – which dominated the scene, although at the end of the day it was the successors of the latter Company who created the climate that led to the demise of the former.

M.J. ARLETT
1986

SR Pacific No. 34041 'Wilton', piloted by class 2P, 4-4-0 No. 40700 cross Tucking Mill viaduct and climb towards Combe Down tunnel with the 12.20 pm (SO) Bournemouth-Nottingham.
B. Ashworth

CONTENTS

My favourite lineside location – and perhaps Ivo Peters' superb photograph can portray better than any words why I considered the view from the stone wall south of Midford viaduct one of the finest on the whole of the S&D. It is late afternoon on 13th September 1958, and the trees cast welcome shade across Twinhoe Lane. But the beauty of the Midford valley remains bathed in sunshine as the 10.28 am (SO) Manchester-Bournemouth, hauled by S.R. Pacific No. 34099 "Lynmouth", and piloted by class 4F 0-6-0 No. 44417, leaves the single-line section from Bath Junction, and begins the 1 in 60 climb past the 'Midford B' ground frame towards Wellow and the south.   Ivo Peters

6

INTRODUCTION

Most railway enthusiasts will claim allegiance to a favourite line. Mine was the 'Somerset & Dorset', the entire line in general, but Midford and the Midford valley in particular. And if pressed to select a favourite lineside location, I have no hesitation in nominating the stone wall at Primrose Hill, south of Midford viaduct.

Over the years I spent so many happy hours leaning or sitting upon that wall that, even today, twenty years after the closure of the line, I can, in my mind's eye, roll back the years – like a film running in reverse. First to disappear will be the trees, which in the years since the closure have self-seeded and grown up along the lineside, and in so doing have obliterated much of the view. Next, the grassy slopes to the embankment and cuttings reassume an air of tidiness. The ballast is no longer overgrown and littered with debris; the track reappears, the rails at first rust red, then the upper surfaces once again glimmering in the sun's rays. Signals and wires come back into view; where paintwork was flaking or bare, colours return; even the little ground frame controlling the single siding, which once again trails into the up line. Finally, the iron bridge that carried the old Great Western branch to Camerton across the lane and under the viaduct. All is again complete. It is time to pause – I am back in the mid-1950s and, of course, it just happens to be a hot, sunny, summer Saturday afternoon.

Time first to regain my breath – it's a very steep climb up the lane, which rises some 200 feet in less than a quarter of a mile. Here, briefly, the routes of rail and road run parallel; the railway climbing at 1 in 60, the lane at 1 in 4, separated from one another by a stone wall. From the road side the wall is barely 4 feet high, but because of the rapidly changing levels between road and rail, the wall is considerably higher on the other side. And, of course, the farther up the lane you climb before looking over the wall, the longer the drop down the other side. So perhaps, with the prudence of hindsight, it is safer merely to lean against, rather than to sit astride, and risk vertigo!

Now to take in the superb view. Just minutes before, when at the foot of the hill, the viaduct dominated the scene, the parapets stretching up to touch the sky. But now I have climbed high above the line and can see the rails sweeping towards the viaduct; the up and down tracks merging to a single set of rails as the imposing eight-arched structure is crossed.

Initially there is little to disturb this picturesque setting; perhaps, because it is summer, the steady drone of a farm tractor as it pulls the hay-turner round and round the meadow down by the stream. Thankfully, the main road on the other side of the valley is still remarkably free of traffic, and in any case, the distance is far enough to drown out most of the noise. Only the occasional heavy lorry might be heard, perhaps a Foden 10-wheeler, labouring in bottom gear up the mile-long climb towards Hinton Charterhouse. Nearer to hand a rustle of wires, and the wooden arm of the tall 'down advanced starting' signal nods earthwards. A down train is signalled, but it will be some 9 or 10 minutes before it appears into view. Suddenly, however, the calm of the valley is shattered. Unheard until now, an up train has drifted around the reverse curves from the south, and has drawn to an involuntary halt at the 'up outer home' signal. The train is still out of sight, but its presence has been betrayed by the sudden eruption of steam from the safety valves. Now a decision. Do I forsake my chosen vantage point, and climb farther up the lane to a point beyond the retaining wall? There, after slipping through the wire fence and crossing a patch of rough grass, I can reach the top of the cutting and obtain a fine bird's-eye view of the up train held at the signal to await clearance of the single-line section into Bath Junction.

No, perhaps it will be best to stay put, for within a few minutes a distant whistle, the sound muffled on the still air, will indicate that the down train has emerged from the southern portal of Combe Down tunnel. At first the passage of the train can be gauged only by a trail of hazy smoke, and even as the grounds of Midford Castle are passed, it is only possible to obtain tantalising glimpses. "It's a double-header!" Now the inevitable guessing game begins. "Is the pilot engine a class 2 or a class 4? Perhaps it's a Bulldog." But even a momentary sighting is sufficient to identify the train's engine. Nobody can mistake the outline of a 'spam-can'. "I suppose it will be 'Wilton' or 'Crewkerne' yet again." (How blasé we used to get – what I would give now to see either engine just once more!)

The train passes under the 'Long Arch Bridge' and finally emerges fully into view, passing Midford station and signalbox before sweeping across the viaduct and onto the double track section to Wellow. Ivo Peters' photograph opposite depicts the very scene, and I make no apology for including a photograph that has previously been published. For no other single picture can better convey the reason why I nominate 'the stone wall' as having been my favourite lineside location.

The engines have been drifting, but are now 'opened out' to attack the 1 in 60 grade. The last carriage has only just disappeared from view when the sound of a whistle indicates that the up train, waiting round the bend, has been 'given the road'. The train comes into view – it's another double-header – this time a class 2P 4-4-0, piloting a Stanier 'Black 5' 4-6-0, a combination of locomotives associated with the S&D since the late 1930s. Both engines are already working hard to gain as much momentum as possible for the steep climb from Midford station up to and through Combe Down tunnel. What a magnificent sight – even more, what a sound – as the exhausts reverberate around the valley long after the train has disappeared from view. Finally a whistle from the pilot engine, and the sound is swallowed up by the tunnel; suddenly, silence returns to the valley.

For many years I had often wondered how many people before me had similarly spent happy hours at this location, watching the trains go by? Then one evening in the early 1960s when enjoying the hospitality of the Midford signalman, an elderly local resident came up into the box. Inevitably talk soon got around to the 'good old days', and it transpired that this old gentleman could recall sitting on 'my' wall as a young boy and watching the GW line being built! And, of course, he could equally recall GW trains passing under the viaduct at Midford, whilst trains resplendent in S&D blue passed over. What a sight that must have been. And, in turn, this old gentleman's father could, no doubt, have recalled seeing the building of the S&D at Midford in the early 1870s. Before then, the lane from Twinhoe took a less direct and more leisurely route around the contour of the hill. Where the stone wall was later to be built was no more than a steep-sloping field, from which the bystander could look down on the old tramway, along which tubs of Somerset coal were horse-drawn from the collieries around Radstock to the canal basin at Midford.

The entire history of the S&D at Midford, from construction to closure, occupied less than a century, and my own recollections little more than a decade. But I count myself very lucky that within that short passage of time, I was privileged to have known the S&D line, and just some of the people who worked upon it.

Believe it or not, this is the same 'view' from the stone wall 28 years later! Mac Hawkins went to great pains (literally!) to obtain this photograph, taken in the Spring of 1986 from the same spot as Ivo's previous picture.

Chapter One
A DESCRIPTION OF THE LINE

This book is about that short but extremely picturesque length of railway which ran from Combe Down tunnel, through Midford, then south past Lower Twinhoe towards Wellow. At times, however, in telling of the local history and the working of the railway, it will be necessary to stray beyond the boundaries of the Midford valley. To describe the route of the line in a meaningful way requires one such foray, but on this occasion only as far north as the junction of the Somerset and Dorset line with the old Midford line at Bath.

Bath Junction and its signalbox lay just ½ mile from the Midford terminus which in later years was known as Bath, Green Park Station. From the junction, which faced towards the terminus, the line began a long sweeping curve which carried the single track of the S&D through

nearly 180 degrees, climbing – with only the briefest respites – at a gradient of 1 in 50. The line passed 2 sidings: May's, serving a brickyard; and the Twerton (later Bath) Co-operative Society, serving a bakery and coal depot – before disappearing, 1 mile 32 chains from the junction, into the depths of Devonshire tunnel. This carried the line under the routes of Wellsway and Devonshire Buildings to emerge, after ¼ mile, into the picturesque and secluded surroundings of Lyncombe Vale.

At the southern end of the Vale, the line crossed a bridge (Bridge no. 14 from Bath junction) which marked the summit of the climb out of Bath. Milepost 2 (measured from Bath junction) was also passed on the bridge; a few yards beyond the line plunged into Combe

A class 2P 4-4-0, and a Stanier 'Black 5' drift down from Combe Down tunnel and across Tucking Mill viaduct with an 11-coach down express to Bournemouth on 22nd May 1956. The wooded surrounds of Horsecombe Vale lead up to the southern rampart of Combe Down, high above the tunnel mouth.
Ivo Peters

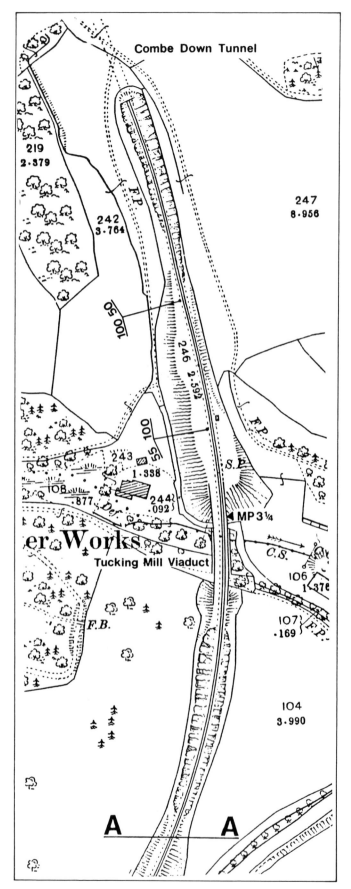

Combe Down Tunnel

219
2·379

247
8·956

F.P.

100 50

242
3·764

246 2·592

F.P.

55 100

243
1·338

108
·877 Def.

244
·092

S.B.

◄ MP 3¼

er Works

C.S.

Tucking Mill Viaduct

106
1·376

F.B.

107
·169

F.P.

104
3·990

A   A

Down tunnel which, like Devonshire tunnel, was extremely restricted and provided very little clearance. The entire length of 1826 yards was completely devoid of any ventilating shafts, giving it the dubious distinction of being the longest unventilated tunnel in the British Isles. The level section from mp 2 extended less than ¼ mile, after which the gradient changed to fall at 1 in 100 until, near the southern end of the tunnel, increasing its fall to 1 in 50.

At 3 miles 5 chains from Bath Junction the rails burst out from the southern portal of Combe Down tunnel into the delightful surroundings of Horsecombe Vale; this in effect is the starting-point of the section of line which forms the main subject of this book. To the lineside observer, the emergence of a train was frequently preceeded, not only by the inevitable rumbling sound and shaking of 'terra firma', but also by a rush of smoke. The bore of the tunnel was so tight that smoke-laden air, displaced by the passage of the train, would be pushed out of the tunnel mouth some moments before the engine appeared out of the gloom!

Immediately beyond the mouth of the tunnel, the sides of the cutting were reinforced by the provision of masonry relieving arches, but so steep was the hillside that within a short distance the cutting gave way to a high embankment. The grade eased briefly to 1 in 100, but within little more than a hundred yards steepened again to 1 in 55 before sweeping past the Midford 'down distant' signal and over Tucking Mill Viaduct (Bridge No.16). Between the tunnel mouth and the viaduct the line passed two lean-to sheds, both situated on the down side. The first shed housed the oil lamps used by the lengthman and gangers when working within the confines of the tunnel. The second hut was the linesman's shed.

Tucking Mill Viaduct carried the line across the wooded Horsecombe Vale, high above the location once known as the Midford Ponds. Below, to the east of the viaduct, lay the buildings of the old fuller's earth works, whose product was, for many years, despatched by rail from the nearby goods yard. From the west parapet of the viaduct, the pump and engine houses belonging to the Waterworks Company could be observed. Milepost 3¼ was passed on the viaduct, after which the line curved through a short, but deep cutting. Here the native Bath stone was exposed by the course of the line.

Emerging from the cutting, the view opened out to reveal, on the up side, the tree-clustered parklands of Midford Castle, whilst on the opposite side the ground fell away towards the disused bed of the old Somersetshire Coal Canal, hidden amongst the trees lining the lane from Midford to Tucking Mill. Yet still further, beyond the lane, Midford Brook meandered towards Monkton Combe and its confluence with the River Avon at nearby Limpley Stoke.

Class 4F No. 44146 pilots SR Pacific No. 34044 'Woolacombe' up the climb towards Combe Down tunnel with a northbound train on 4th August 1951. This was the Saturday preceding the August Bank Holiday and in 1951 some seven up and six down relief trains ran in addition to the normal busy summer Saturday service.   Ivo Peters

A pair of class 4F 0-6-0s emerge from the cutting south of Tucking Mill viaduct and sweep down the bank towards Midford with the 10.38 am (SO) Manchester-Bournemouth train on 23rd August 1952. The 1 in 55/150 gradient post throws a shadow onto the ballast in the foreground.   Ivo Peters

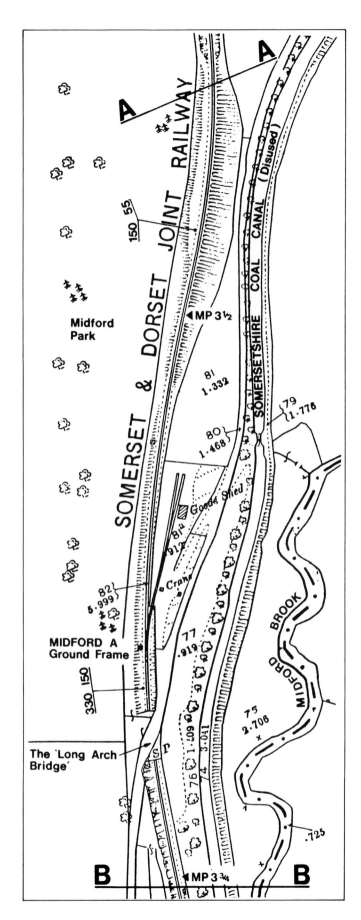

Known to local S&D men as the 'Park Bank', the extremely picturesque stretch of line, southwards from the cutting at Tucking Mill, crossed the lower reaches of the castle parklands on an embankment which, because of the lie of the land, was far higher on the down side than on the up. Just before reaching mp 3½ the gradient of the line changed to 1 in 150 down. Here, on the approach to Midford goods yard, the curvature changed, the line passing another permanent way hut, this time sited on the up side.

The yard, on the down side, comprised only two sidings, access to which was controlled by 'Midford A' ground frame, sited on the opposite side of the line. The goods shed, with its semi-circular roof clad in galvanised corrugated iron and boarded timber walls, resembled more a farm building. At the south end of the yard a crane was provided, and here the two sidings merged into one before passing under a loading gauge sited just inside the white-painted gate which was kept closed and secured across the line into the yard.

On passing the yard, the line entered a short cutting and the gradient eased still further to 1 in 330 down, as the line burrowed under the Tucking Mill lane. This crossed the line at an oblique angle and resulted in the overbridge (Bridge No.17) taking on the appearance of a short tunnel, some 37 yards in length. High above the line, on the ground over the 'Long Arch Bridge' (the official title of this bridge) were the Midford 'down home' and 'wrong road' signals.

Immediately to the south of the 'Long Arch Bridge', the line emerged to run along the steep hillside on a narrow ledge, passing mp 3¾ and, on the down side, yet another timber-built linesman's shed.

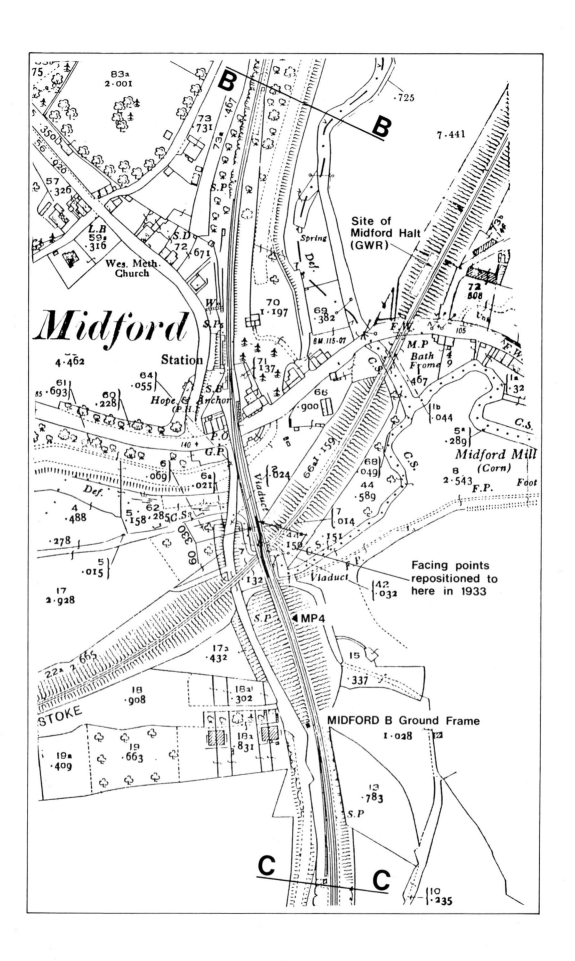

75

83a
2·001

73
731

.467

.725

7·441

73a

S.P

350

56 920

57
·326

S.D
72 671

L.B
59a
·316

Wes. Meth.
Church

Midford

Site of
Midford Halt
(GWR)

Spring

Def.

72
808

70
1·197

69
382

F.W.

Station

4·462

64
·055

71
137

66
900

BM. 115·07

M.P
Bath
Frome
·467

105

F.W.

61
693

85

60
·228

Hope & Anchor
(P.H.)

S.B

68
·049

44
·589

C.S.

1b
·044

5a
·289

C.S.

1a
·32

2

6
·069

6a
·021

140

P.O.

G.P.

Viaduct

·024

Midford Mill
(Corn)

8
2·543

F.P.

Foot

Def.

5
·158

62
·285

C.S.

4
·488

5
·015

·278

60 330

7

44
150

C.S.

7
151

7
014

Facing points
repositioned to
here in 1933

17
2·928

132

Viaduct

42
·032

MP4

S.P

15
·337

22a 2·665

17a
·432

18
·908

18a
·302

MIDFORD B Ground Frame
1·028

STOKE

18a
·831

13
·783

19a
·409

19
·663

S.P

C

C

10
·235

The north end of the station platform lay just south of the 'up starting' signal. The single platform, on the up side of the line, was far longer than necessary to meet the latter-day traffic needs at Midford. At this end, the platform was devoid of any buildings other than a lean-to shed which served as the oil store and lamp room. The main station building, constructed in timber, was near the southern end of the platform, whilst high above the line was 'Hazel Elm', the stationmaster's house.

As the line curved through the station it continued to hug the hillside. Opposite the platform, the ground fell away in a precipitous descent towards the bed of the old coal canal, some 40 feet below the line. Here, along the side of the track, a wooden guard fence was provided. A very fine view could be obtained from the platform, particularly north-eastwards along the valley towards Monkton Combe. Beyond the cottage rooftops on the opposite side of the brook lay the overgrown track of the old GW branch line running on an embankment, but at a much lower level than the S&D.

Leaving Midford station, the line passed the 'down starting' signal and the lineside apparatus used to retrieve the Bath Junction to Midford single line tablet. Another standard, for the delivery of the tablet to an up train entering the single line section, stood on the opposite side of the line in front of the signal box. A range of wooden sheds, housing the permanent way trolley and trailer, stood just beyond the box on the northern end of Midford viaduct, an eight-arch structure which carried the line high across the Bath to Frome main road, the dried up bed of the canal, and the Limpley Stoke-Camerton branch line. The latter, in turn, passed over the Cam Brook at the point where the waterway passed under the S&D viaduct.

Two-thirds of the way across the viaduct the gradient changed from 1 in 330 down to 1 in 60 up. This point also marked the end of the single-line section, 3 miles 76 chains from Bath Junction, the facing points leading to the start of the double track section which extended southwards for 32½ miles to Templecombe No.2 Junction. At the far end of the viaduct the line ran onto a high embankment passing mp 4, opposite which stood the 'up inner home' signal. Also on the up side was another small ground frame, known as 'Midford B', which controlled access to a single siding trailing into the up line.

Midford station and signalbox framed, on the left, by the 'down starting signal' (later to be replaced by the Western Region of BR), and, on the right, by the very distinctive 'Wrong-road' signal.
R.C. Riley

BR class 4, No. 75073, heads southwards past the signalbox on 1st September 1962, and is about to regain the double track section. Note that when the signalbox was rebuilt in 1936, the original stonework to the lower part of the rear wall was retained, but the upper part was rebuilt in brickwork. In the background, the lane to Twinhoe passes the derelict arch of the GW Camerton branch, before climbing past the gate which, until 1960, gave access to the up siding.   B.J. Ashworth

The backdrop to Midford, looking at its best. S.R. Pacific No. 34107 'Blandford Forum' heads south with a down 'Pines' relief on 7th June 1958.   Ivo Peters

A lightweight load for S&D class 7F 2-8-0, No. 53807 – one of the large-boilered 1925 series – seen here passing the up siding on a dull day in March 1951. The catcher arm is extended ready to pick up the pouch containing the Midford-Bath Junction single-line tablet.

Ivo Peters

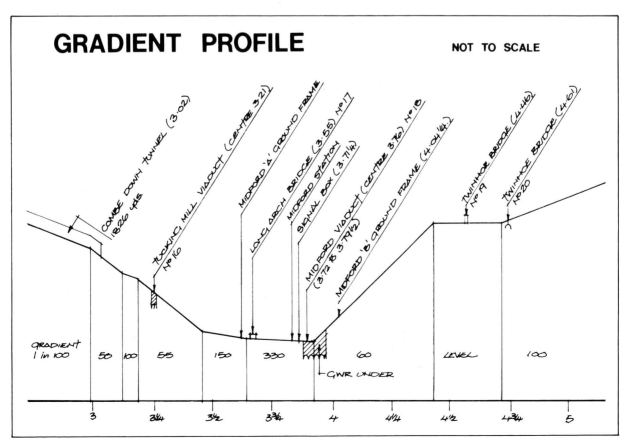

GRADIENT PROFILE

NOT TO SCALE

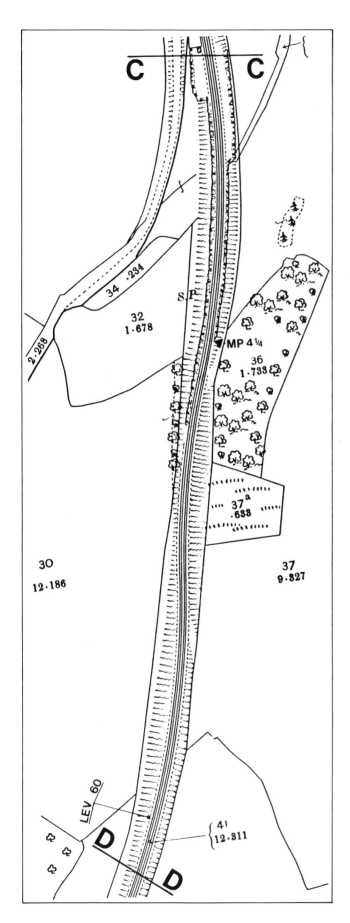

Opposite page top: Class 4F 0-6-0, No. 44146 assists SR Pacific No. 34107 'Blandford Forum', as they head southwards from Midford with the 9.10 am (SO) Birmingham-Bournemouth on 10th August 1957. On the up line, class 2P No. 40698, and SR Pacific No. 34043 'Combe Martin' are held at the Midford 'up outer home' signal waiting for clearance of the single-line into Bath with the 9.55 am (SO) Bournemouth-Leeds train. *Ivo Peters*

Now the line curved into a deep rock cutting passing the very tall 'down advanced starting' signal. The first of the lineside permanent way huts south of Midford station was immediately behind the buffer stops at the end of the up siding. Here a high wall retained the lane from Midford as it climbed towards Twinhoe and Wellow. Continuing through the rock cutting, the line passed, on the up side, the 'up outer home' signal where, on summer Saturdays, many a northbound train was brought to an involuntary halt awaiting clearance of the single line section into Bath. Below, and affixed to the same post as the 'outer home' was a calling-on arm, officially entitled the 'shunt by outer home signal', which, when pulled off, enabled a train to be drawn forward towards the 'inner home'. (In more than a decade, I only saw this signal used once!)

On the approach to the mp 4¼ the line briefly assumed the route once taken by the coal canal tramway which carried coal from the Radstock collieries to the canal at Midford. Southwards from Midford the line passed through the superb rolling countryside by a succession of reverse curves. The rock cutting led to a short embankment which, in turn, reverted to a cutting before the line finally surmounted the 1 in 60 climb from Midford viaduct followed by a brief section of level track, passing mp 4½ and curving under Twinhoe Bridge. Provided in 1892 when the section of line between Midford and Wellow was doubled, this bridge (No.19) served as an accommodation crossing for use by the farmer at Lower Twinhoe House.

Opposite page bottom: BR class 9F 2-10-0, No. 92205, with the 9.55 am (SO) Bournemouth-Leeds, drifts around the curve past the 4½ milepost and starts the 1 in 60 descent towards Midford. The Level/60 gradient post can just be seen behind the left-hand front buffer of the locomotive. The date was 30 July 1960, and No. 92205 was one of four BR9s allocated that year to the S&D for the duration of the Summer service. *Ivo Peters*

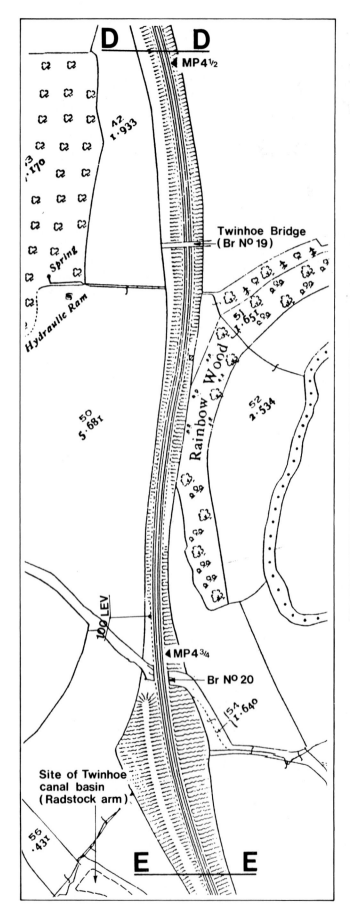

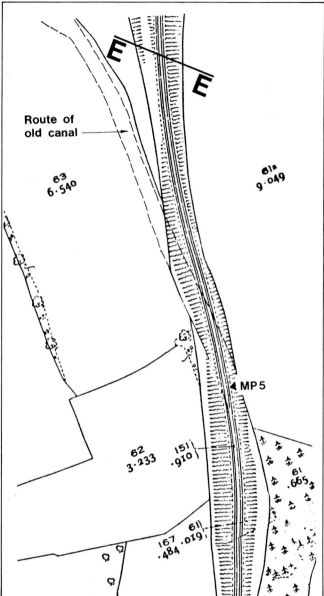

Once again the curvature of the line changed, skirting a crescent-shaped strip of woodland, appropriately named Rainbow Wood, and passing another permanent way hut, the last within the length of line under the control of the Midford Gang. Nearing mp 4¾ the line climbed again, this time at 1 in 100 onto an embankment and across an overbridge.

Bridge No.20 was, like nearby No.19, officially entitled 'Twinhoe Bridge' and carried the line over what was, long ago, a drove-lane between Twinhoe and Wellow. Any possible confusion arising from both bridges bearing the same name was overcome, at least by Ivo Peters, who rechristened Bridge No.19 'Edward's Bridge', a reference to a long-standing friend, Col. E. Trotman, who for many years lived at Lower Twinhoe Cottage, overlooking the line.

S&D class 7F 2-8-0, No. 53806 passes under Bridge No. 19 – 'Twinhoe Bridge' – and skirts Rainbow Wood near Lower Twinhoe with the 5.00 pm down goods from Bath on 11th May 1957. The permanent way shed on the right was renewed towards the end of the 1950s.   Ivo Peters

Beyond this bridge, nearly a mile from Midford station, the 'up distant' signal was passed. Here, hidden from view behind a hedgerow on the up side of the line, a depression in the corner of a field marked the site of what was once the basin of a canal, along whose placid waters Somerset coal was carried from Radstock, for trans-shipment at Twinhoe into tubs which in turn were hauled down the tramway to the main canal at Midford.

Here also, where the line passed mp 5 and turned into a deep cutting to skirt Hankley Wood, is the southern limit of that length of the S&D which this book covers.

Class 4F No. 44135 and BR5 No. 73087 are in charge of the 10.38 am (SO) Manchester-Bournemouth on 18th July 1959, and are about to cross Bridge No. 20 which, like No. 19 seen in the background, was officially referred to as 'Twinhoe Bridge'. The 4F is passing the 4¾ milepost, whilst on the right, almost hidden from view but level with the rear of the tender of the BR5, is the gradient post marking the end of the level section of line, which now begins to climb again, this time at 1 in 100.   Ivo Peters

The Midford Valley – looking southwards from Lower Twinhoe – the railway sweeps across Bridge No. 20 (Twinhoe Bridge), and around the reverse curves towards Wellow. On the down side, just before reaching the bridge, the 4¾ milepost can just be seen. Hankley Wood lies to the left of the point where the line disappears from view, whilst the hedgerow in the right background separates the railway from the route of the old Radstock-Twinhoe arm of the coal canal. An SR Pacific, running light-engine – passes Midford 'up distant' signal. The photographer is standing close to the site of the canal tramway, the route of which crossed the field in the foreground.   Col. E.A. Trotman

Class 2P 4-4-0 No. 40698, and S&D class 7F No. 53803 climb the 1 in 100 grade away from Lower Twinhoe towards milepost 5 and Hankley Wood, with a southbound train. The basin of the long-disused Radstock to Twinhoe arm of the coal canal was located behind the hedgerow on the left.   Ivo Peters

Chapter Two

MIDFORD BEFORE THE RAILWAY

Midford c.1870. A view looking westwards across the valley before the railway age reached Midford. To the right is the canal weigh-house erected by the Somersetshire Coal Canal Company. The large detached dwelling prominent in the centre of the picture was the canal toll collector's house. Further to the left stands the 'Hope and Anchor' and beyond the cottages soon to be demolished to make way for the erection of the new railway.   Collection Dr. L. Smith

The small village of Midford lies at the confluence of two brooks, the Cam and the Wellow, which come together to flow north-eastwards, as Midford Brook, towards the river Avon near Limpley Stoke. The rolling valleys through which these waterways meander represent some of the finest scenery to be found in the area immediately to the south of Bath, which is separated from the Midford valley by the massive bulk of Combe Down, rising to over 500 feet.

Midford cannot even lay claim to a parish of its own, straddling instead the boundaries of five separate parishes and two counties, for here a tongue of Wiltshire tumbles down the hillside to meet what was once 'smiling Somerset', but is now the County of Avon. Along the brooks lie the evidence of early industry, the remnants of small corn and fulling mills. There was little, however, to

relate about Midford in the early guide books of Somerset. Indeed, until the construction of Midford Castle around 1775, there appears to have been no event, nor any buildings of sufficient merit to warrant any mention. Midford Castle is reputed to owe its origins to the gambling successes (in particular one very substantial win at cards) of Henry Roebuck, for whom it was built. Allegedly, the castle was built in the shape, when viewed from above, of the Ace of Clubs!

From high upon the hillside, the owner was able to look down across the newly planted parkland, and enjoy the uninterrupted beauty of the valley. What, one wonders, was the reaction when, less than 20 years later on 17th April 1794, the Somersetshire Coal Canal Company obtained Parliamentary approval to construct a canal? This waterway was to extend from a junction

Midford c.1920. Although it is jumping well ahead of the period covered in this chapter, this photograph, taken from a similar position to the previous one but some 50 years later, makes an interesting comparison, showing both the S&D and, nearer the foreground, the GW Limpley Stoke to Camerton line. The canal weigh-house, demolished in 1914, has been replaced by 'Lynwood', a house which features in a later chapter. The old toll collector's house, 'The Moorings', is little changed whereas the 'Hope and Anchor' is now cloaked with ivy.   Collection Dr. L. Smith

A tranquil scene – reputed to be the Somersetshire Coal Canal looking west from Midford, and showing a pair of barges heading towards the locks at Combe Hay.   Collection Dr. L. Smith

with the Kennet & Avon Canal at Dundas in the Limpley Stoke valley, passing but a ¼ mile below the castle lawns, and through Midford village to Timsbury in the Cam valley. At Midford, a branch was planned to extend southwards, through Twinhoe and the Wellow valley, to the coalfields of Radstock and Welton.

Construction of the canal proceeded apace, but it was not until November 1801 that through traffic began over the entire length of the Timsbury Basin to Dundas section. The delays had been caused by difficulties west of Midford, where the lie of the land necessitated a considerable change in the levels of the canal. After costly trials, following the construction of a Caisson lock (which was, in effect, a type of boat lift), the lower and upper levels of the canal were finally linked by an inclined plane. Even this method proved to be a costly mistake and, by April 1805, it was replaced with a flight of 22 conventional locks.

There were also problems on the Radstock arm of the canal, caused by a dramatic change in levels just south of Midford. The junction for this arm, at Midford, was completed in 1803, as was a 60 foot long aqueduct

The remains of the Radstock arm of the SCC which, until replaced by a tramway, terminated at a basin near Twinhoe. The bed of the canal can be traced, running parallel with the hedgerow on the right, to the site of the basin in the far corner of the field in which the photographer is standing. The trackbed of the S&D can be glimpsed at a lower level through the trees towards the right of the photograph.   Mac Hawkins

carrying the canal over the Cam brook. From a basin on the south side of the brook, a flight of 19 locks was planned to lift the canal to the upper level, which had already been completed as an isolated section between Twinhoe and Radstock. (The course of this section of canal would, nearly 70 years later, influence the route to be taken by the S&D). The bottom lock, together with the basin at Midford, were completed when, possibly as a temporary measure, it was decided to link with the upper level near Twinhoe by means of a mile-long tramway.

The tramway was completed by 1804, but thereafter the Radstock arm appears to have seen little regular use. The necessary transfer of coal from canal to tramway at Twinhoe, and back into barge at Midford, must have proved a deterrent to trade, especially when coal from the nearby Cam valley could be moved without any such trans-shipments.

In 1815 the problem was finally overcome by abandoning the Radstock to Twinhoe canal section and substituting a tramway along the canal towpath. This

new tramway, some 7 miles in length, and built to a gauge of approximately 3′ 5½″, enabled a team of three horses to haul a load of eight or nine wagons. From the end of the old canal section near Twinhoe, the tramway no doubt took up the course of its predecessor, following the contour of the hillside to cross, on the level, an old drove-lane below Lower Twinhoe House. From this point, the tramway descended towards the basin at Midford, passing around the hill which formed the headland separating the valleys of the Wellow and Cam brooks. Passing loops and laybys were provided at regular intervals along the route of the tramway; three between Twinhoe and Midford. Mid-distance between these points a trough was also provided for the horses employed in hauling the coal trucks. Apparently the tramway also provided a more direct benefit to the villagers of Midford, for it has been suggested that at weekends the coal wagons were swept clean and, with wooden boards serving as 'seats', carried passengers to market at Radstock!

Pre-S&D Modes of Transport

Left: The Somerset Coal Canal looking north towards Upper Midford. Beyond the bridge, the canal turned eastwards (to the right, as viewed) and headed towards Midford village.

Right: The canal barge weigh-house at Midford, erected by the SCC Company in 1831. The route of the S&D ran through the trees on the left. A once familiar sight – but now almost forgotten – a hayrick, built adjacent to the canal towpath, along which the horses are 'posed' for the benefit of the cameraman.

Left: The Bath to Frome turnpike road. On the left, the 'Fox Inn' – Midford's second public house, which boasted a 'Skittle Parlour' (alley). In later years the GW branch-line to Camerton would span the road a little farther beyond the buildings on the left. In the foreground, the wheelmarks of horse-drawn traffic are clearly visible. The 'Fox' has long-since closed and the carriageway is today somewhat busier! All photos: Courtesy Dr. L. Smith.

26

By 1820, in excess of 100,000 tons of coal were passing through Midford each year, and just seven years later the villagers might well have been startled by the appearance of a 'locomotive steam carriage', brought into use to haul trains of coal along the tramway to Midford. This locomotive, designed and built by William Ashman, Engineer at Clandown colliery, unfortunately proved too heavy for use on the lightweight rails of the tramway, and was soon relegated to serve as a stationary engine at Clandown.

A few years later, in March 1831, the Canal Company erected a barge-weighing machine immediately below the point where, 43 years later, Midford station would be built. The next quarter of a century saw the Somersetshire Coal Canal flourish, but by the 1840s a new rival form of transport – the railway – began to threaten the prospects for future trade along the canal. The first direct challenge came with the opening, on 14th November 1854, of a broad-gauge mineral line, 8¼ miles long, connecting Radstock with the GWR at Frome. Even so, the canal initially retained a near-monopoly of coal transport. Many a local railway scheme was proposed over the next decade or two, often in attempts to break this stranglehold on trade. But the first scheme directly to

affect Midford was proposed by the proprietors of the canal to construct a broad-gauge line from Radstock to join the GW line to Bath, north of Limpley Stoke. Plans for this 'Radstock & Bath Railway' were deposited on 30th November 1864. The main route was planned to start from a point close to the Bell Inn at Radstock and to follow – as far as was practical – the route of the canal tramway towards Midford. Here the line would descend at a gradient of 1 in 100 to cross the Wellow brook and the turnpike road from Bath to Frome, and continue along the valley past Monkton Combe to join the GW line at Dundas. The overall length of the proposed line was 8 miles 2 chains, but in addition, a loop 4 furlongs in length was planned to connect to the GWR at Radstock, whilst at Bath, another short branch was projected to leave the GW line near Hampton Row and to terminate immediately south of Cleveland Bridge, where the Bath Fire Station stands today. In the event the Bill was withdrawn upon the threat of a proposed line from Camerton to Bath, which would have competed for trade on the main arm of the coal canal.

One scheme which did eventually succeed was for the Bristol and North Somerset Railway, the construction of which was planned to link Bristol and Radstock.

This view of the trackbed of the S&D, looking towards Midford from the south, shows the point where the line, when constructed in 1872/4, cut the route previously taken by the SCC tramway, which followed the gap through the trees on the right.   Mac Hawkins

Authorised in 1863, the Company was to struggle for 10 years before finally opening the line to traffic on 3rd September 1873. Meanwhile, the Midland Railway had reached Bath in 1869, and the occupants of that city, always one of the major markets for Somerset coal, were able to take advantage of cheaper prices of coal brought in by rail from the collieries of the Forest of Dean and the Midlands. A greater threat was posed by the plans announced by the Somerset & Dorset Railway Company in 1871 to construct an 'Extension line to Bath' linking their existing system from Burnham to Wimborne, at Evercreech, with the new Midland line at Bath.

The extent of any local reaction at Midford to these proposals is largely unrecorded. But it is known that the owners of the Midford Castle Estate were to prove a thorn in the side of the S&D. Whether the owners, in presenting a petition to the House of Commons, were directly opposed to the line passing through their estate, or merely taking action to ensure that they obtained the best possible deal from the Railway Company, is unknown. If the latter, the owners of the Estate more than succeeded in their aims, for in an Agreement dated 20th April 1871 the following were just some of the conditions accepted by the Railway Company in return for the Estate withdrawing all opposition to the Bill, and selling to the S&D some 10 acres of land, together with an easement for a tunnel, at a price of £5,500:

> Subject to Parliamentary or Board of Trade requirements, no permanent signals or sidings shall be erected between certain points on the land.
> All telegraph posts shall be arranged so as to be as inconspicuous as possible, and shall always be kept painted green.
> The slopes of the embankment in the valley through the Midford Ponds shall be properly soiled and the Company shall well plant on both sides with ornamental shrubs and shall preserve and replant the same as and when necessary.
> The Company shall construct and always maintain a suitable archway and sluices or floodgates for the passage of water from the Upper to Lower Ponds. Another cutting at least 14 feet high by 12 feet wide with paled oak double entrance gates to be constructed and maintained by the Company for afford-

ing access from the lane near Tucking Mill to Priory Woods.
> The Company to erect and maintain on both sides of the Railway through the Park a wire fence with iron standards with oak field gates plus a level (occupational) crossing with gates.
> As many trees as possible to be maintained standing.
> The route of the railway through the Park may deviate south of the centre line shown on the deposited plan but not north [ie: no nearer to the castle buildings].

These were just some of the many 'conditions' imposed. The S&D also agreed to make, and maintain, a passenger and goods station in Midford village, and were granted the right to take additional land at or near the south (Midford) end of the proposed (Combe Down) tunnel at the rate of £200 per acre for a further station.

The Railway Company obtained the necessary Parliamentary approval on 21st August 1871. This Act – The Somerset & Dorset Railway (Extension to the Midland Railway at Bath) Act – gave the Company powers to raise £360,000 by the issue of new shares, and to borrow a further £120,000. Authority was also provided to purchase the tramway at a cost of £20,000, for the proposed railway was to follow, as far as was possible, the route of this tramway between Midford and Radstock.

Contracts for the construction of the new line were placed with Messrs. Charles & Thomas Walker of Westminster, and work commenced early in 1872, under the direction of Consultant Engineer W.H. Barlow, with Mr. A. Priestley as the contractors' Chief Engineer. The works in the vicinity of Midford were amongst the heaviest on the entire line, including the construction of the Combe Down and Bloomfield (Devonshire) tunnels. The former occupied about 18 months, working from both ends towards the middle where, despite the length and restricted bore, the separate workings were only a matter of inches out of alignment when they finally broke through to join up under Combe Down. At the deepest point, towards the southern end, the tunnel is some 350 feet below ground level. Originally, other than at each end, it was considered unnecessary to provide a continuous masonry lining.

South of Combe Down tunnel, work on the viaducts at Horsecombe Vale and at Midford was advancing well by the end of 1872, with the abutments, together with some of the piers, already erected. Both structures were major engineering works, built in local limestone, no doubt obtained from the deep cuttings and tunnel

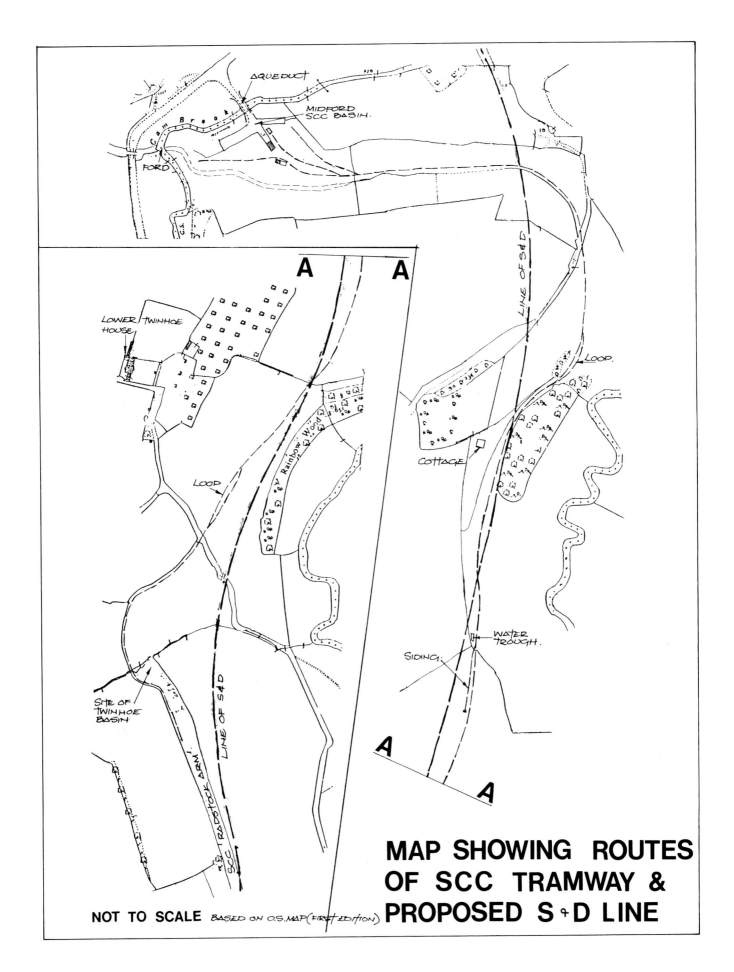

AQUEDUCT

MIDFORD
SCC BASIN.

Cam Brook

FORD

A A A

LOWER TWINHOE
HOUSE

LINE OF S&D

LOOP.

Rainbow Wood

LOOP

COTTAGE

SITE OF
TWINHOE
BASIN.

SCC RADSTOCK ARM

LINE OF S&D

WATER
TROUGH.

SIDING.

A

A

**MAP SHOWING ROUTES
OF SCC TRAMWAY &
PROPOSED S & D LINE**

NOT TO SCALE BASED ON O.S. MAP (FIRST EDITION)

workings. Tucking Mill viaduct consisted of eight arches with an overall length of 96 yards and a maximum height of 63 feet from ground to rail level.

North of Midford, the line was taken under the lane to Tucking Mill and Monkton Combe by means of the short 37 yard tunnel, again constructed in masonry with a span of 14′ 10″ and a height of 13′ 11″ from rail level to soffit of arch. Two deep cuttings were required – formed by blasting through the solid Bath stone. The first, only a few chains in length, lay immediately to the south of Tucking Mill viaduct. The second, being both longer and deeper, lay south of Midford viaduct, taking the line through the brow of the hill to gain the alignment of the old canal tramway, which it crossed and recrossed before reaching Twinhoe. Here, south of Midford viaduct, the new line cut across the route of the old lane from Twinhoe, which had to be diverted. Much of the land hereabouts was in the ownership of William Gore-Langton, the local MP and Lord of the Manor. Until the coming of the railway there had been no direct access from the Twinhoe lane, across the river and canal to the turnpike road, other than by a circuitous route, which involved fording the river, via the Combe Hay lane. As part of the Agreement for the sale of his lands to the railway company, the latter constructed a new length of carriageway parallel with the railway viaduct, crossing both the Cam Brook and the canal to join the main road opposite the access to the new station.

The station site and the approaches were formed on a narrow shelf hewn out of the steep hillside, along which the new formation ran from the Tucking Mill lane overbridge to Midford viaduct. The station buildings were, unlike others provided on the new line, of timber construction, and access to the station was provided immediately parallel to the viaduct.

The entire line extended 25¾ miles, climbing from near sea-level at Bath to over 800 feet in crossing the Mendips near Masbury. To survey a railway through such terrain was in itself no mean task. But with eight major viaducts and tunnels totalling nearly 1½ miles in length, the completion of the line within just two years, whilst still an outstanding feat, was regrettably achieved at the expense of adequate standards of workmanship. The contractor engaged as many as 3,000 hands on the work, and the costs eventually exceeded £400,000.

In April 1874, with the work approaching completion, the contractors threatened to withdraw all labour, and to abandon all work still outstanding, for the S&D was no longer able to meet the contractors' costs in cash payments. A compromise was reached with Messrs. Walker accepting shares as part payment, and with the balance of their costs met in Lloyds' Bonds. This action, together with the suspension of all work not considered essential for the opening of the line, enabled works to proceed, and in June 1874, application was made to the Board of Trade for the necessary Certificate authorising use of the line for public travel.

The Board of Trade inspection was undertaken by Col. Rich who, from 25th to 27th June, examined and tested the various bridges, viaducts and other works. The Inspector was obviously far from satisfied with much of what he saw, noting the inadequate means of drainage, the improper repair of earth slips, and poorly constructed bridges and viaducts. "The pier in one large viaduct," he reported, "is 6 or 8 inches out of perpendicular." He also determined that the permanent way in the Combe Down tunnel was to be lifted and relaid.

Various remedial works were undertaken, and on Friday 17th July, a further inspection was undertaken. This time Col. Rich was prepared to recommend approval, but only subject to qualification. He reported that "the works on this railway are very heavy and have not been executed with the care that they should have been." His report concluded with the recommendation that "all [of the works] must be carefully watched for some years to come".

Upon at last receiving the necessary Board of Trade Certificate, the railway company immediately announced their intention of opening the line with effect from the following Monday – the 20th July 1874.

Above: Tucking Mill viaduct, showing the eastern face as originally built in 1873/4. The photograph – one of a set – was taken to show the widening of the viaduct in 1891/2, but the works have yet to encapsulate the existing arches and parapets. S&D No. 35, a Johnson 'Scottie' 0-6-0 locomotive built in 1878, is seen crossing the viaduct with a southbound train.

Right: Tucking Mill viaduct, again in the early stages of widening, but showing the structure as originally built, wide enough to accommodate only a single set of rails. The steam crane is shown, lowering one of the timber centres, a supply of which can be seen stacked next to the lineside at the north end of the viaduct. The parapets show no sign of recent disturbance in which case that on the right seems somewhat low! The original distant signal, the rear face of which is just visible, is also of interest.

Left: Tucking Mill Viaduct. Part of the western face, as originally constructed, and looking northwards towards Combe Down.
All photos: S&DR Trust, Courtesy Reg Randell

This photograph must have been taken c.1900, after the widening of Midford viaduct, but before works commenced on the construction of the GW Camerton branch line, the route of which would pass under the third arch nearest the camera. The view shows all of the original signalling in the vicinity of the station, including the subsidiary arm (3 push) on the same post as the 'down starting' signal.

Collection Duncan Harper

Chapter Three

1874-1929: YEARS OF CHANGING FORTUNES

The inaugural train from Bath left the Midland station at 7.25am on Monday, 20th July 1874. The *Bath Chronicle* report noted that "very few passengers went by it. Possibly comparatively few were able to avail themselves to it at such short notice". Unfortunately no reference is made as to whether the arrival of this train at Midford, at approximately 7.40am, was greeted by any special celebrations, such as those noted at nearby Wellow and at certain other stations down the line, which resulted in the train reaching Templecombe well after the connecting service to Exeter had departed!

What use the would-be travellers of Midford made of their new railway is uncertain. Perhaps the local advantages are best summed up in the following extract from a charming publication, *The Somerset & Dorset Railway. Tourists' Descriptive Guide*, by D.H. Gale, published in 1874 by James Keane in celebration of the opening of the Bath extension:

> The substitution of a short and comfortable journey of half-an-hour between Radstock and Bath, for a couple of hours crawling over formidable hills, cannot fail to attract a greater number of visitors to this city on ordinary as well as on special occasions.... The viands and beverages of which we diurnally partake must show that there is a close alliance between the wants and interests of town and country. Those who manufacture cheese and butter and raise vegetables, will find their time economised and their products enhanced in value by the existence of a more expeditious means of transit.

In the harsh world of reality, the S&D Railway Company had provided the opportunity for local people to benefit from the new era of communication whilst at the same time the Company itself, not for the first time, stared bankruptcy in the face. There was insufficient revenue to meet the payment of dividends and the maintenance costs of the new line. Similarly there were no capital reserves left to finance investment in much-needed new rolling stock, or in the provision of the additional sidings and other works needed to

accommodate the growth of traffic. The only course of action, other than to lapse into bankruptcy, was to sell the line, and this was eventually achieved by means of a 999 year joint lease to the Midland Railway (with whom the S&D connected at Bath), and the London & South Western Railway (with whom the S&D connected at both Templecombe and Wimborne).

Whilst these financial problems were possibly of but passing interest to the villagers of Midford, an event which occurred just 5 miles south of Midford during the following year was to cause great local concern. On Bank Holiday Monday, the 7th August 1876, two trains met in head-on collision near Foxcote, between Wellow and Radstock. The crash, which occurred at about 11.20pm, resulted in the tragic loss of thirteen lives, with many more injured. The two trains involved were both specials: the up train a relief from Wimborne, whilst the down train had been run primarily to collect some 300 members of the Bath Young Men's Liberal Association from Midford, where they had attended a fête. The latter train had already passed south through Midford, intending to run the stock to Radstock, where the engine was to have run round, and returned the train to Midford to collect the large contingent of passengers waiting to travel home to Bath. In the event, their train was never to arrive and after a long wait, news of the accident filtered through to the crowded platform at Midford and the homeward journey was made on foot.

What facilities were originally provided for the intending passenger at Midford is unclear, but by the Autumn of 1876 the newly appointed Joint Committee for the railway had approved plans for 'improved passenger accommodation'. The following year witnessed the first of many representations for the erection of a goods station. Following refusal by the Company, another such request was made in 1878, but again it was indicated that the Joint Committee "was not prepared to incur the cost of purchasing the necessary land".

Towards the end of 1878 traffic was disrupted as a result of difficulties with the Combe Down tunnel, which on 21st March the following year claimed the life of a platelayer run over by a train. The tunnel must have continued to cause problems, for on 3rd August a labourer was injured by falling scaffolding. A different problem arose on 14th August 1880, when an object was found on the line between Midford and Wellow, evidently placed there "for the purpose of throwing a train off the rails", proving, perhaps, that vandalism is not a modern phenomenon! During the same year the Joint Committee

Doubling of the line
1. Tucking Mill viaduct
(S&DR Trust, courtesy Reg Randell)

Left: Widening of the pier separating spans 5 and 6 in progress, showing the scaffolding and hoist. As with Midford viaduct, the widening was undertaken on the west (up) side of the original structure, which was encased in brickwork.

Below: Work nearing completion – a photograph taken from the north end. The rock cutting to the south is yet to be widened out. Was the bowler-hatted gentleman the foreman of the works, I wonder?

The completed work as seen from the down side of the line.

Widening in progress in the deep cutting immediately to the south of Tucking Mill viaduct. The contractor's temporary narrow gauge track is visible to the right of the single-line.

35

Works in hand on the widening of Midford viaduct in 1891. Work on each arch from the near (southern) end is progressively more complete than the next, so that whilst the scaffolding has already been removed from the nearest span, at the far end work is still at an early stage. To the extreme left, immediately above the cottage roof, the end of the station canopy is visible. The signalbox, however, is yet to be built.

2. Midford viaduct Doubling of the line
(S&DR Trust, courtesy Reg Randell)

The viaduct, as widened, from the east side, with the original masonry structure now encased and strengthened with brickwork. The signalbox has now been erected, and can be seen at the far end of the viaduct.

received a request to improve the wooden bridge on the road across the canal. This was the bridge erected by the S&D in 1873/4 to carry the diverted lane from Twinhoe over the coal canal at the side of Midford viaduct. The original bridge restricted passage of all but the lightest of traffic, and the railway Company was informed that an iron replacement span would cost £550. Consideration was thus deferred, but in the event the local Highway Board refused to take over the maintenance of either bridge or roadway unless the former was rebuilt! The Joint Committee relented and an order was placed for the new bridge. (It still stands today.)

immediately to the north of Midford. On the first occasion, a wagon belonging to the Babbington Coal Company broke loose, causing the derailment of twelve other wagons, and considerable damage to the track. The second time, it was another private owner's wagon, this time belonging to the Butterley Company, which left the rails, damaging three other trucks and S&D brake van No.27.

At the end of 1886, the area around Bath was hit by some extremely severe weather. Heavy falls of snow destroyed much of the telegraph route between Bath Junction and Wellow, and the single-line tablet instru-

The completed structure showing the west (up side) face as viewed from the Bath road in 1892. In the foreground is the iron bridge spanning the coal canal which, since 1890, had traded at a loss leading, in 1893, to the liquidation of the canal Company. Note the new 'up inner home' signal, bolted and braced to the face of the viaduct.

In 1883, yet another request was made for siding and goods accommodation, this time by the Fuller's Earth Company who owned the works at nearby Tucking Mill. Again the request was rejected. Passengers were obviously faring better, for at the beginning of 1884 plans were approved for lengthening the station platform, further improvement being made when the 'waiting shed' was closed in at an estimated cost of £14.

In the early years, Midford appears to have witnessed its fair share of minor derailments. On 21st January 1885, for example, a coal wagon belonging to the Midland Railway Company left the rails approaching Midford, and on the 14th July in the same year, a wagon axle broke on the 6.25pm down goods. Twice during 1888, on the 3rd February and 5th June, the 8.30pm goods train from Bath to Templecombe was derailed

ments were put out of action for three days from 9pm on 26th December, requiring pilotman working.

In November 1890, the S&D Joint Committee requested the L&SWR to seek powers to widen various sections of the single line, including the length between Midford, Wellow and Radstock. The necessary Act of Parliament was obtained by the L&SWR on 21st July 1891, and included powers to extend the double line northwards from Midford, to a position close by the southern end of Combe Down tunnel. The Joint Committee appears to have decided to restrict the extent of works north of Midford station to the widening of Tucking Mill viaduct, and opening out the cutting immediately to the south. The estimated cost was £12,000, excluding the purchase price of any additional land.

Work began on the doubling of the line late in 1891. Both Tucking Mill and Midford viaducts were widened by the erection of new structures abutting the west face of the original viaducts. The workmanship of 1872-74 had already given rise for concern, especially at Midford where two of the slender masonry piers had been previously encased in brick. The remainder of the original masonry to both structures was similarly encased, this reducing the span of each arch by 9 inches, with further strengthening achieved by adding brick rings to each arch and buttressing some of the piers. Three cottages, fronting the Frome road, were bought for £500 plus fees, and appear to have been substantially rebuilt. Part of the cottage nearest the viaduct seems to have been demolished to provide working space for the widening works, and the remainder of the cottages converted, or possibly rebuilt as two dwellings. Evidence of such work still survives in the form of the timber bargeboards on the western gable, an exact match of the pattern which adorned the once nearby signalbox. A new access road was built, as the original now lay under the foundations of the new viaduct. (This today serves as the entrance to the car park to the Hope & Anchor Inn.)

South of Midford viaduct, the new works required the opening out of the deep cutting close to the Twinhoe lane, including the construction of a high retaining wall on the west (up) side of the line. This meant another minor diversion of the lane at Primrose Hill, whilst a short length of the carriageway south from the bridge over the Cam Brook was raised and regraded. The works enabled an access to be provided from the lane to a single siding laid in on the up side of the line.

At Lower Twinhoe, an existing farm crossing was replaced by an overbridge. Officially this bridge became known as 'Twinhoe Bridge' (4 miles 46 chains from Bath Junction) and was typical of many overbridges built by the S&D for 'occupation' access to farm land, constructed of wrought iron girders and corrugated floor plates supported on masonry abutments. Twinhoe Bridge was built with a span of 25 feet and a minimum headroom of 13' 9" from rail level to underside of girders. Just 15 chains to the Wellow side of this new bridge, the existing underbridge carrying the line over the lane below Lower Twinhoe Farm was widened. Here, a new brick arch supported on masonry abutments was built on the north (up) side of the original bridge which in turn was strengthened with brickwork.

The widening of the line was to claim the life of one labourer when, working between Midford and Wellow on 29th November 1891, he stepped from the new formation onto the original single line and was struck down by the 8.30am Evercreech - Bath passenger train.

The line through Midford now required full signalling, so a signalbox was erected at the north end of the viaduct, close to the end of the station platform. The

new works were inspected on behalf of the Board of Trade by Major Yorke, on 27th August 1892. He recommended that the faces of the overbridges should be dressed back to ensure a clearance of at least 2' 4" from the side of the widest vehicles using the line. The Inspector commented that "In the case of Midford viaduct, which is close to the station, it is necessary that handrails of sufficient height be fixed on the tops of the parapets to prevent passengers, who may leave the carriage by mistake before reaching the platform, falling over the viaduct." He further suggested that the line through the station be doubled and an additional platform provided. These latter proposals, which would have involved heavy engineering works at an estimated cost of £7,000, were at once rejected, and the position of the facing points leading into the double-line section was

Midford signalbox c.1900, showing the original access and verandah which were altered c.1905 following the introduction of the Whitaker automatic tablet exchanging apparatus.

Collection Colin G. Maggs

to remain at the Wellow end of the station platform, immediately to the north of the new signalbox. The Midford to Wellow double line section was opened to traffic on 28th August 1892.

Over many years an established trade from Midford was the despatch of fuller's earth (a type of clay primarily used for 'fulling' cloth) which, before the opening of the railway siding, must have been transported from Midford by barge via the old coal canal. From the workings at Odd Down, close to the southern boundary of Bath, the 'earth' was hauled by horsedrawn wagons to the head of Horsecombe Vale, north of Midford. Here it was transferred into tubs and worked down the hillside, using a self-balancing inclined tramway. After washing, the clay was dried, refined and bagged up in the Fuller's Earth Works at Tucking Mill, and finally carted to the railway siding south of Midford viaduct.

During 1893 the Agent, engaged by the Railway Company to haul the fuller's earth, complained of the heavy grades from Tucking Mill to the goods siding and threatened to withdraw his services unless the haulage rate was substantially increased. Obviously by this date the Joint Committee placed greater credence on the potential traffic than had been the case in earlier years, for the minutes of an Officers' Meeting of the Joint Committee on 23rd January 1894 noted:

> ...a plan was submitted showing how siding accommodation, with a suitable approach road, can be afforded midway between Midford station and Tucking Mill for dealing conveniently with the fuller's earth &c., conveyed to and from the district, and it is anticipated that the establishment of this Depot will attract stone and other traffic to the Joint Line, and also render unnecessary the continuance of the special charge now paid by the Joint Committee for haulage. It was agreed to recommend that the work be carried out at an estimated cost of £780, exclusive of the necessary land.

An early view showing the north end of the station, with a down mixed train approaching the platform. Note the station nameboard which, in later years, was renewed and sited further along the platform towards the lean-to lamp room and oil store.

Collection Duncan Harper

It was pointed out that the Company already possessed the powers necessary to acquire the land, which fell within the 'limits of deviation' of land required for any future doubling of the line between Midford and Combe Down tunnel. Just under one acre of land was purchased for the construction of the small goods yard which opened to traffic following a Board of Trade inspection on 21st December 1894. Situated on the down side of the line, just north of the 'Long Arch Bridge', access from the single line was controlled by a small lever frame housed in a timber-built hut with a slate roof erected on the opposite side of the line. The covered goods shed, and the 6 ton capacity crane, were probably provided at this date, although neither was shown on the plan submitted to the Board of Trade.

In 1894, it was realised that the powers obtained under the L&SWR Act of 1892 for the compulsory purchase of land north from Midford station towards Tucking Mill viaduct would soon lapse. Notices to Treat were therefore served and a strip of land on the west (up) side of the line, northwards from the 'Long Arch Bridge' appears to have been purchased at this time. An area of land had already been allocated in Horsecombe Vale, between Tucking Mill and Combe Down tunnel, for the future provision of a small 'halt' to serve the residents of Combe Down, and possibly Monkton Combe. But although, as already noted, the expense of widening Tucking Mill viaduct and of opening out the deep cutting through the rock south of the viaduct had been incurred in anticipation of extending the double line, further work never proceeded. Possibly it might have been the anticipated traffic and operating difficulties in starting heavy northbound trains on adverse gradients just before entering Combe Down tunnel which deterred the Company from widening the Midford to Tucking Mill section in isolation from the remainder of the line into Bath Junction. And, in turn, it was the horrendous costs of widening Combe Down and Devonshire tunnels which acted as the barrier to doubling this latter section. In 1904 the Joint Committee noted that "there was still no immediate probability of doubling the Bath-Midford single line in view of the very heavy outlay in forming a second tunnel through the Combe Down hill." The passage of time and the inflationary years during and following the First World War ensured that the opportunity to double this section of line was lost forever.

Between the opening of the S&D extension to Bath, and the late 1880s, trade on the old coal canal had steadily declined. In 1893 the Canal Company finally passed into liquidation, with closure following in November 1898. In the Cam valley, to the west of Midford, a 3½ mile branch line, connecting Camerton with the Bristol & North Somerset line at Hallatrow, had been opened on 1st March 1882. This line provided direct rail access to the Camerton coalfield and led to a further reduction in the volume of traffic carried by the canal.

Between 1891 and 1896 the S&D refused to consider various local proposals for the construction of a branch railway connecting the collieries east of Camerton to the S&D at Midford. In 1902, however, a scheme was promoted under the title of the North Somerset Light Railway. The route of this line, surveyed by the engineering firm J.H. Rhodes of Leeds, was planned to run from Greyfield Colliery, near Clutton, via Camerton and Midford, to connect with the Great Western line at Dundas. The costs of the proposals were estimated to an incredibly precise sum of £134,563 2s 3d, which included a connection with the S&D at Midford. The deposited plans showed that the line would approach Midford from the west on a high embankment before running on to a viaduct, 277 yards in length. This would carry the rails over the lane to Twinhoe, under the S&D viaduct, before crossing – in turn – the Cam and Midford brooks and the Bath to Frome main road. The connection to the S&D, which included a second viaduct 42 feet high and 110 yards in length, would terminate with a connection to one of the sidings in Midford goods yard.

The promoters found little support, the scheme being opposed by the Great Western Railway Company and the Light Railway Commissioners, for not only would the railway compete for traffic with the existing Camerton to Hallatrow line, but the route would seriously interfere with the workings of a colliery near Camerton.

In the same year, 1902, Midford figured in another abortive scheme – the Bristol, London and Southern Counties Railway. Linking Bristol and Avonmouth with the L&SWR at Overton, near Basingstoke, this scheme included proposals for a branch line, about one mile in length, from Monkton Combe to Midford. The Bill promoting this railway was thrown out of Parliament on 9th June 1903.

An amended North Somerset Light Railway scheme – this time prepared by engineers S.W. & A.L. Yockney of Westminster – was promoted in 1903. These new proposals involved a line from the S&D at Midford, passing via Combe Hay and Dunkerton, to Priston and included a short branch line west of Dunkerton. Despite proposing the use of the bed and tow-path of the old coal canal wherever possible, the route required a ruling gradient of 1 in 40 for the climb out of the Cam valley towards Priston. At Midford, the junction with the S&D was planned immediately to the north of the 'Long Arch Bridge' facing towards Bath. This would have enabled traffic to be run into the adjacent goods yard. The actual point of divergence from the S&D appeared, however, to be south of the S&D overbridge, for there was no reference on the plan to widening out the 'Long Arch Bridge'.

These amended proposals were, as in 1902, opposed

ABORTIVE RAILWAY SCHEMES
1864-1903

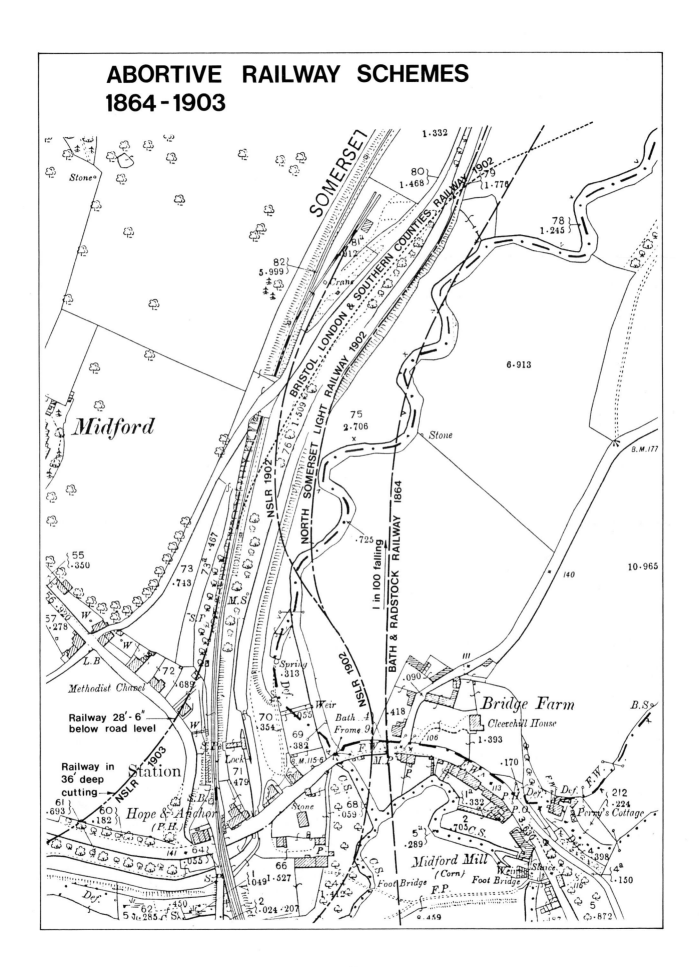

by the GWR who, during an Inquiry held at the Guildhall in Bath, announced their intention to apply for powers to extend their own line from Camerton, by way of Midford to Limpley Stoke. The following year the GWR purchased the coal canal from the Liquidator for the sum of £2,000. Any opposition from the promoters of the North Somerset Light Railway was bought out by a payment of £500 and the promise to support any scheme for a line between Priston and the proposed GW line at Dunkerton.

Plans were next drawn up for a connection between the proposed GW branch and the S&D at Midford. The proposals included extending the double line section from Wellow northwards through Midford station, which would be completely rebuilt with two platforms. The new spur connecting with the GW branch line would diverge immediately north of Midford viaduct and fall south-westwards at a gradient of 1 in 100 to form a facing connection towards Combe Hay. New signalboxes would be required at the north end of the rebuilt S&D station and at the proposed junction with the GW line meaning that the existing S&D box would be demolished as it stood on the line of the junction with the new spur. The proposals also envisaged the enlargement of the S&D goods yard together with the provision of exchange sidings on the up side of the single line, within the parkland of Midford Castle. Like all previous, and indeed subsequent, proposals for a connection between the two lines, the scheme failed to materialise.

Above: Johnson 0-6-0 'Bulldog' No. 63 waiting to leave Midford with an up train. Built at Derby Works in 1896, No. 63 survived (as LMS No. 3198) until December 1947.
L&GRP, courtesy David & Charles

Below: Johnson 4-4-0 No. 17 pauses for custom with a down train. No. 17 was built at Derby in 1891, and was withdrawn by the LMS (as No. 302) in June 1932. L&GRP, courtesy David & Charles

Although of poor quality for reproduction, a fascinating photograph taken from the S&D viaduct and showing early work on the construction of the GW branch line. The contractor's locomotive and two trucks can be seen, together with some temporary track. On the extreme left is the south face of the canal bridge, this being the only known photograph showing this bridge. The large house on the right must have been less than 30 years old, but lay on the line of the proposed railway, and would soon be demolished.

Collection Dr. L. Smith

Construction of the Limpley Stoke to Camerton branch line was let in 1906, the old coal canal, over the route of which much of the new railway was to run, having been drained the same year. The line opened to traffic on 9th May 1910. At Midford the new line extended through a deep cutting west of the village, before passing onto an embankment to cross over the Cam Brook and, further east, the Midford to Twinhoe lane immediately before passing under the S&D viaduct, for which privilege the GWR were charged an annual easement plus a compensation payment of £125. As the GW line ran under the S&D, it recrossed the Cam Brook, whilst a little further to the north-east the new line crossed over a triple-arched brick viaduct, one span of which bridged the Midford Brook. Immediately beyond, a steel-plate girder span carried the line over the main Bath to Frome road. Just to the north, a halt was opened by the GWR on 27th February 1911 to serve Midford which could now boast TWO stations! Midford Halt remained open for just four years; for on the 22nd March 1915 passenger services over the GWR line were withdrawn as a wartime economy.

The years leading up to the First World War were the peak of prosperity for the S&D, with both freight and through passenger traffic flourishing. Even so, the Officer Minutes for the period indicate that Midford continued to figure prominently amongst the inevitable minor 'irritants' which tend to bedevil any organisation. Examples include the following:

On 20th July 1911 a bundle of barbed wire, having rolled down the slope in the grounds of

Midford Castle, burst through the iron fence separating the park from the railway just as the 2.22pm express passenger train from Bath was passing. The wire caught underneath the first van and was carried a considerable distance, with the result that some crossing sleepers were dislodged and several chairs broken, in addition to some slight damage to the van. The cost of the damage has been defrayed by the owner of the wire...

The sum of £20 has been paid to Mr. J.S. Collins in respect of damage by fire to a plantation of young fir trees alongside the line at Midford on 2nd March 1914, allegedly due to one of the Committee's engines...

On 3rd November 1914, when the 5.48pm passenger train was approaching Bath, the connecting rod on the engine broke. The accident occurred on the single line from Midford and some delays to trains resulted.

With the outbreak of war, the line was to serve as an important military link with an ever-increasing volume of munitions and other war materials carried by rail over the Mendip Hills to the south coast ports. The railways emerged from the war years to face new threats – the increasing competition of road transport, especially local motor bus services, and years of economic depression and escalating costs.

Passenger services were belatedly restored to the GWR Camerton branch on 9th July 1923, but the little Halt at Midford was to remain closed and was later demolished. Just two years later, passenger services over the line were again withdrawn, this time for good, the last passenger train running on 21st September. Earlier the same year, on 30th May, Dunkerton colliery had closed and despite a subsequent and very brief resurrection, during which a small amount of coal was again wound, only one daily freight working was now necessary to serve the sole remaining colliery at Camerton.

In the early 1920s, a coal merchant's business, Hamlen & Sons, was established at Midford goods yard, and over the next forty years, first the horse-drawn wagons and, later, the brown liveried lorries of Messrs. Hamlen were a familiar sight in the lanes and villages around Midford. Coal was brought in by rail from both the Radstock collieries, and from the North of England and, in addition to household deliveries, Hamlen & Sons supplied the Waterworks Company at Tucking Mill and the Malthouse at Midford. The carriage of fuller's earth to the goods yard, was also contracted to Hamlen's, over 200 tons being despatched by rail on some weeks.

As a result of the Railways Act of 1921, the railways of Britain were, in 1923, amalgamated into 'The Big Four'. The Midland Railway became one of the constitu-

Midford in September 1922.

A rare view showing the double-track section from Wellow which extended across the viaduct from 1892 until 1933, and the signalbox in original condition. The Limpley Stoke-Camerton branch line can be seen crossing the lane to Twinhoe and heading westwards towards Combe Hay.   Collection George Dow

44

Midford in September 1922 showing the signalbox as built in 1892 other than the alterations to the access steps; the station complete with full canopy; and the tall starting signal. The original position of the facing points leading to the double-line section can be seen immediately to the north of the signalbox. This was the position selected in 1892 when the line to Wellow was doubled.   Collection George Dow

ents of the London, Midland & Scottish Railway, whilst the other joint owner of the S&D line (the L&SWR) formed part of the new Southern Railway. The LMS and Southern Railway Companies now became 'joint owners' of the S&D line, which was, however, initially allowed to continue under a separate management. But the costs of operating the line were still escalating, and dramatic and urgent reforms were obviously necessary. As early as 1922, an independent report on economising had been called for. Locally, the duties of the station-masters at Wellow and Midford were to be combined, the Wellow station-master, Mr Moors moving into the station house at Midford later in the 1920s. Soon more radical changes

would take place, leading to the demise of the famous prussian blue livery of the locomotives and coaching stock of the S&D.

Against this gloomy background a tragic accident occurred on 20th November 1929, when the driver and fireman of a heavy northbound goods train were overcome by fumes as their engine laboured up through the smoke-filled Combe Down tunnel. Out of control, the train ran away down the long 1 in 50 approach to Bath Junction. The train negotiated the junction points but crashed at the entrance to Bath goods yard, killing the driver and two other railwaymen.

Local Passenger 1936: ex-MR 0-4-4T No. 1387 passes the up siding with a local passenger train bound for Bath in 1936.   L&GRP courtesy David & Charles

Local Passenger 1959: class 2P 4-4-0 No. 40698 drifts across Midford viaduct with a Templecombe-Bath stopping train on 6th July 1959. This photograph was taken from the trackbed of the old GW Limpley Stoke-Camerton line, the rails of which had been lifted the previous year.   R.C. Riley

Chapter Four

1930-1966: THE YEARS OF DECLINE

2P 4-4-0 No. 568 crosses the imposing Tucking Mill viaduct with a Bath-Templecombe stopping train complete with vintage L&SWR 3-coach set. Around this period, the brick refuges on both viaducts at Midford were removed to be replaced by iron guard rails. The resultant 'making good' to the brickwork is clearly visible.   Ivo Peters

On 1st July 1930 the separate management of the S&D was discontinued, the line now coming under the direct control of the LMS and Southern Railway. In one way or another, this was to prove an eventful decade in the railway history of Midford.

On the GW branch the line between Hallatrow and Camerton had been closed and the track lifted in 1933. In June 1931 the Limpley Stoke-Camerton line was used in the vicinity of Camerton for the filming of scenes for Arnold Ridley's classic, 'The Ghost Train', whilst in

November 1937 the film-makers returned to the line to record scenes for the Edgar Wallace thriller, 'Kate Plus Ten'.

Meanwhile, alterations were taking place to the layout of the trackwork on the S&D at Midford. As part of a programme of works the facing points leading from the single-line section were re-sited from just to the north of the signalbox, to a position towards the southern end of the viaduct. This work, undertaken on 9th April 1933, enabled a speed restriction imposed in the up direction to be relaxed.

More dramatic, but totally unplanned alterations took place three years later when, at 10.06am on Wednesday, 29th July 1936, the calm of the Midford valley was shattered by the actions of a runaway engine, devoid of both driver and fireman and propelling a rake of eight empty coal trucks. The origins of this escapade took place some 5½ miles south of Midford, at Braysdown between Wellow and Radstock. Here, the 8.10am Evercreech-Bath freight train hauled by S&D class 7F 2-8-0 No.13803 over-ran signals and all but collided head-on with an 0-6-0 'Jinty' tank No.7620 which had been busily engaged on shunting duties at the sidings serving the Braysdown and Writhlington collieries.

The crew of the up train, fearing a collision, had jumped from the footplate of No.13803 with the intention, it was later stated, of attempting to pin down the brakes on the passing goods wagons. The driver of the shunting engine, noting only at the last moment the approaching freight train, reversed his own engine before he too jumped down from his footplate. From the ground he now noticed that the freight engine was slowing, and managed to mount the footplate and successfully halt the train.

Meanwhile, however, the fireman on the 'Jinty' had also 'baled out' from the cab! No.7620, with a good head of steam and a fully opened regulator could now be observed rapidly disappearing from view in the direction of Wellow. One can well imagine the feelings of the enginemen!

As soon as the Braysdown signalman saw the engine set off, he sent the 'train running away' emergency bell signal to the adjoining box at Wellow. This he followed up with a telephone message, informing his colleague that there was nobody on the footplate of the errant engine. Signalman Banfield at Wellow had insufficient time to take any action, for No.7620 had made good time and stormed through Wellow station and past the box, propelling the eight empty trucks at an estimated speed of 50mph.

Signalman Larcombe was on duty at Midford box, and had barely received news of the incident, when the 'runaway' hove into sight around the curve south of the viaduct. He shouted a warning to Stationmaster Tinney, who wisely sought refuge on the floor of his office.

The points controlling access to the single-line into Bath Junction were set and bolted for the 'down' line, and as the wheels of the leading truck struck these points, the wagon was derailed. Within seconds, this truck hit the signalbox, partially wrecking the masonry base, and causing considerable damage to the locking frame and superstructure. Signalman Larcombe, although badly shaken, fortunately escaped injury.

What happened next was graphically described by the reporter of the *Bath Chronicle & Herald*:

The train continued its headlong career for a few yards, where the trucks came into contact with the end of the platform. Wooden railings were smashed, and debris from the vehicles hurled along the platform. A wooden panel of a door was smashed out; a platform truck had a portion of an end smashed off; a stout timber from a truck went through a side of the wooden packing case, a buffer with a piece of truck was thrown onto the platform, which was littered with broken timber.

Meanwhile even more dramatic happenings were taking place on the offside. The signal post was snapped off like a carrot and fell down the bank, where it lodged about half way. Derailed trucks went "over the top", crashing through trees and undergrowth, growing on the bank, smashing some completely. A large portion of the stone wall was carried away

with falling trucks on to the gardens beneath, as well as much of the ballast from the side of the permanent way. Telegraph wires were snapped like string and the pole near the station looked as though it had been struck by a tornado.

'Lynwood', a house which nestles at the foot of the embankment, 30 feet or more below the station, had a remarkable escape as 'bits of truck' crashed down the bank.

It was just like a thunderbolt said Mr W.H. Berry, a visitor to the house, who was inside the porch as blocks of stone and fragments of metal and wood were hurled into the garden. One piece of iron went through the slate roof... another missile smashed through one of the windows near the porch, narrowly missing the parrot, and the dog only just avoided the avalanche of wreckage that crashed to the lawn.

Despite the track having been severely damaged, the engine and one truck somehow kept to the rails. This remaining truck started to break up just north of the station, and portions of the body and underframe were distributed along the next 300 yards of the track; one pair of wheels were later found alongside the line under the 'Long Arch Bridge'. The remainder of the truck, now running on just one pair of wheels, was pushed a further distance of three miles, passing through the Combe Down and Devonshire tunnels. Finally, directly beneath the Claude Avenue underbridge, the end door of the truck fell off and jammed under the wheels of the engine, thus finally derailing No.7620, and bringing an end to the escapade.

Meanwhile back at Midford all was in chaos. The crash, which had been heard up to a mile away, had drawn a crowd of villagers to the station. The signalbox structure was leaning towards the station approach road, which was littered with debris. All communication with Wellow and Bath Junction signalboxes had been destroyed, but notice of the runaway was relayed to Bath via the public telephone.

A 1938 view showing one of the Stanier 'Black Fives', newly allocated to Bath to work over the S&D, assisted by class 2P No. 635 climbing away from Midford with a southbound express.
L&GRP, courtesy David & Charles

Within an hour of the crash, gangs of men were being sent out to repair the track. So expeditious was the work of clearing and restoring the line that, by 7.00pm, just nine hours after the crash, traffic resumed over the line by pilotman working. The rebuilding of the signal-box, together with the replacement of damaged equipment, of course took considerably longer.

Much of what remained of the signalbox was demolished. The masonry base housing the locking frame was rebuilt, but the original superstructure was replaced by a 'temporary' timber and glazed structure with a flat roof, which survived 30 years, until closure of the line in 1966! The lower flight of the access steps together with the wooden quarter landing, both severely damaged by the crash, were also rebuilt in brick and concrete.

Mercifully, there was no injury (other than perhaps to pride) nor any loss of life and, as such, the incident has come to be looked upon, in retrospect, with some amusement. How different things might have been if the incident had occurred just minutes later, when a passenger train was due to leave Bath. Had the two trains met head-on between Bath Junction and Midford, possibly within the confines of Combe Down or Devonshire tunnels, the results would have been horrendous. But for once fortune smiled upon the S&D. (By a remarkable coincidence noted by the *Bath Chronicle*, there happened to be a notice displayed at Midford station on the day of the crash advertising a showing in Bath of 'The Ghost Train' which, of course, had been filmed only 5 years earlier on the GWR line at Camerton, just a few miles to the west of Midford!)

Yet more changes would soon be noticed at Midford, for north of Bath the LMS Company had authorised a programme of bridge renewals and strengthening on the line from Mangotsfield, whilst at Bath motive-power depot an enlarged turntable was installed. These works, when completed by 1938, at last enabled heavier, more powerful locomotives access onto the S&D line and on 2nd May 1938 Stanier Class 5, 4-6-0 locomotives – the famous 'Black Fives' – entered regular service over the Mendips, including haulage of the S&D's premier train, 'The Pines Express'.

Left: A down train emerging from the 'Long Arch Bridge' in 1936 hauled by 2P 4-4-0 No. 699 assisted by 4F 0-6-0 No. 4274.

Right: S&D 2-8-0 No. 13804 storms past the tall 'up starting signal' and climbs towards the 'Long Arch Bridge' with a heavy up freight train in 1937.
All photos L&GRP courtesy David & Charles

Left: 2P No. 623 and 4F No. 4557 climb away from Midford with a down express bound for Bournemouth on a hot Summer day in 1936. Note the wagon standing in the up siding – not an everyday sight, even in pre-war years!!

Soon, however, the outbreak of the Second World War in 1939 led to the disappearance of all through express trains, whilst local passenger services were dramatically curtailed, the line also reassuming military significance. The heavy air raids on Bath, early in 1942, left undamaged the Midland & S&D lines into the city. During the nightly bombing, however, many people sought refuge in the comparative safety of Midford and the surrounding villages.

Peace brought renewed changing fortune to the two railways of Midford. If proposals put forward by the planners in Bath had come to fruition, the railway network around Midford would have been considerably changed. As part of the post-war redevelopment of Bath, it was proposed to close the existing Midland and Great Western stations and to construct a new 'Central' station. The LMS and GW lines, which ran parallel towards the western approach to the city, were to be linked north of Newton St Loe, and all traffic would use the new station to be sited near the Bath West goods yard. East of this, a new line was to diverge from the GW line, turning southwards and tunnelling under the eastern end of Combe Down to emerge just east of Monkton Combe. Here, a triangular junction was to connect, north of Limpley Stoke station, with the GW line to Bradford on Avon and, via the old Camerton line, to the S&D just south of Midford viaduct. At Midford these proposals would have required a short but steeply graded spur connecting the formations of the GW and S&D lines which would have enabled the S&D Midford-Bath Junction single-line section, and the GW Bathampton-Limpley Stoke section to be closed (by-passing the notorious and expensive to maintain Combe Down and Devonshire tunnels and easing considerably the heavy gradient encountered on the climb from Bath Junction to Combe Down tunnel).

The planners found no favour with the railway companies, but surprisingly, less than four years later, in February 1947, the GWR resurrected the scheme, discussing it with the Bath planners! In the event, the scheme was overtaken by the nationalisation of the railways; but it is interesting to note that the proposals were not finally abandoned until the latter part of the 1950s.

The Transport Act of 1947, resulting in the nationalisation of Britain's railways, saw the S&D line initially assigned to the newly-formed Southern Region of British Railways. But the S&D was one of those 'penetrating lines' which crossed the boundary between the Western and Southern Regions of the new regime. So within two years the commercial, but not the operating, control of Midford and the northern half of the line passed to the Western Region.

'The beginning of the end?' In 1958 the Western Region of British Railways finally gained total control of the northern half of the S&D line. On 29th October 1958 Mr K.W.C. Grand, general manager of the WR, made a tour of inspection. The special 2-coach train is seen halted at Midford where stationmaster Bob Ryan greets Mr Grand and other officers, including (with hand on hips) Mr Reggie Hanks.

Photo courtesy Mrs M. Ryan

Meanwhile the Camerton branch line had become an insignificant and totally uneconomic part of the WR. On 14th April 1950 the last coal was wound at Camerton and this last remaining colliery in the Cam Valley was closed. By the Autumn of that year, one train per month was sufficient to transport what little freight traffic was left. Closure of the line followed inevitably the following year, the last train running to Monkton Combe only, on 15th February 1951. All was not quite dead, however, for in 1952 the branch line was selected as the location for filming what has now become the classic railway comedy, 'The Titfield Thunderbolt'. Several sequences of this film were shot at Midford, including the opening scene, a train hauled by Bulleid light Pacific No. 34043 'Combe Martin', passing southwards over Midford viaduct, followed by a train, GW 0-4-2, No.1401, emerging from under the viaduct on the Camerton line. The scene, lasting only a few seconds on film, took considerably longer to shoot! After several weeks, which witnessed the star of the film, the very elderly locomotive 'Lion' (temporarily renamed 'Thunderbolt') trundling to and fro along the line, the film crews departed. It was six years later, however, before the track along the branch was recovered in 1958, following which the steel bridge-spans

over the Twinhoe lane, the Cam Brook and the main Frome road were removed for scrap.

By the 1950s few people made use of the local passenger service from Midford. The station had originally served a catchment area which extended far beyond the village boundaries but, by now, those people who did not yet own a motor car, chose to travel by the more convenient bus service. But if local rail travel languished, the same could not be said of the through traffic, which throughout the 1950s ran on summer Saturdays in a seemingly endless stream of trains carrying holiday makers to Bournemouth from the industrial towns and cities of the Midlands and North of England.

In 1953 Midford station, signalbox, and the ground frames received the attention of the WR painters, and the old Southern colours of green, cream and white disappeared under a new, and unwelcome, hue of brown and cream; a visual reminder that commercially the WR was now firmly in control. At the same time the station canopy was removed.

In 1958 the WR finally gained total control of the northern section of the S&D line and there now began the sad, but well documented, decline which was to lead, within eight years, to the closure of the railway. The first

GW 0-6-0 OPT No. 9612 crosses over the Midford to Twinhoe lane with a demolition train on 15th February 1958.   Ivo Peters

The same train as seen from the main Bath to Frome road. Here No. 9612 propels the train westwards from Midford towards Combe Hay. The train was used to recover track and fittings as the GW line was lifted.   Ivo Peters

positive sign of retrenchment at Midford could hardly have been unexpected; the closure in June 1959 of the up siding which, in post-war years, had been very little used. The siding was subsequently removed together with the small ground frame, 'Midford B', which had controlled access to the siding.

At the beginning of 1958 the parapet walls on Midford viaduct were completely rebuilt, including new guard rails. Most of the work was undertaken on Sundays when no regular traffic ran over the line.

In early December 1960, following a period of exceptional rainfall, the city of Bath and the surrounding areas suffered the worst flooding since the 1880s, with river levels 17 to 20 feet above normal. At Midford the formation of the line immediately north of the station collapsed, carrying away a section of the embankment and track-bed, where the line ran along the narrow ledge cut into the hillside. The line was closed for several days whilst gangs of men reinstated the embankment and track ballast. This operation provided the rare sight of at least one heavy ballast train arriving from Bath with an S&D class 7F 2-8-0 locomotive at both the head and rear

of the train. Approaching the 'Long Arch Bridge', this ballast train was brought to a halt and the single line tablet given up by the driver of the leading engine in order to release the 'A' ground frame. The leading engine was then detached from the train, run forward and set back into Midford goods yard, clear of the running line. With the points reset for the main line, the other class 7F locomotive at the rear of the train was able to propel the ballast trucks under the 'Long Arch', to the point of the slip.

Fortunately the slip occurred on a winter Sunday when the S&D line was closed to traffic. However, disruption was considerable, with local and semi-fast passenger trains to and from the south terminating at Radstock, which involved some long 'tender-first' working. Freight and coal traffic to and from the Radstock area had to make a long detour southwards, and production of coal was affected by delays in obtaining enough coal trucks. On at least one occasion, it was reported that the old connection between the S&D and GW yards at Radstock, was used, an operation possible only by passing through Ludlow's colliery! The 'Pines Express'

During January 1958 the parapets on Midford viaduct were rebuilt and new guard rails erected. Most of the work was undertaken on Sundays so as not to disturb normal traffic. Here the engineers' train has been propelled onto the up line, clear of the single-line section, which enabled a BR Standard Class 4 to run out from Bath to relieve the class 4F 0-6-0 and her crew.   Ivo Peters

was diverted at Broadstone, via Ringwood, Salisbury, Westbury, Bath Spa, Bristol Stapleton Road and Filton Junction to regain the normal route to Birmingham at Yate South Junction. On one occasion, Monday 5th December, a Bulleid light Pacific, No.34102 'Lapford', worked through from Bournemouth to Birmingham New Street, returning next day with the southbound working. The line through Midford was eventually re-opened in time to be used by the down 'Pines' on Friday 9th December.

Just occasionally, excursion trains over the S&D were worked by Diesel Multiple Units. One such working was on Sunday 21st August 1960 with a Cheltenham-Bournemouth excursion which slowed at Midford to enable the single-line token to be given up by the driver to the signalman.

Courtesy Mrs M. Ryan

In the Spring of 1962 British Railways announced that all through holiday trains, together with 'The Pines Express', were to be re-routed away from the S&D line at the end of the Summer timetable working. Thus Saturday 8th September 1962 witnessed the final passage of 'The Pines' and all of the other holiday trains through Midford. On the previous day the Midford stationmaster, Keith Cooper, set up his tape recorder inside the signalbox and recorded the passage of the penultimate down 'Pines'. The entire sequence, from the moment that signalman Charlie Eyre accepted the train from Bath Junction, to the giving of the 'train out of section' bell code provides a poignant record of the passing of the S&D's most famous of trains.

Overnight the S&D had effectively become little more than a local 'branch line', carrying few passengers other than by way of the very occasional excursion. Obviously local traffic alone could never sustain retention of the S&D on economic grounds. At Midford, for example, the gross takings for passenger and parcels traffic over a six month period spanning 1962/63 totalled just £80. But now it was the turn of coal and freight traffic, on which the line had in previous years so long prospered. Now this traffic was, seemingly deliberately, being run down to a minimum by diverting traffic to other routes.

In June 1963 Midford goods yard was closed and the two sidings were lifted, leaving the crane to stand sentinel before it too finally succumbed to the oxy-acetylene torch of a local scrap merchant. In September 1964 the line closed at night for the first time since the opening of the railway in 1874. As a result, Midford box had to lose one 'turn' and Charlie Eyre, having been 'last in' was 'first out', transferring to the box at Limpley Stoke over the hill in the Avon valley.

In February 1964 Midford station was reduced in status to that of an 'unstaffed halt'. Last redecorated in 1953, the station had always been well-maintained, but now an air of neglect crept in as paintwork began to flake and peel – the all too sad image of a dying railway. The following eighteen months saw dates for closure first rumoured, then announced only to be deferred. But in September 1965 consent to close the line with effect from 3rd January 1966 was confirmed. Ironically, perhaps on reflection sadly, this date had to be yet again deferred due to the late withdrawal of one of the companies chosen to provide the regulation alternative bus service. The reprieve was, however, to be short lived, and closure finally came on Sunday 6th March 1966. Over that weekend it was estimated that more than 2000 people travelled over the line in special trains. Perhaps if more of them had used 'the Dorset' the line might just have survived – but somehow I doubt it. At Midford many people waited at the station and along the lineside to record on film, or merely to watch in sadness, the passing of those last trains and the end of an era.

A sad occasion: the last up Pines Express to pass over the S&D bursts out of 'Long Arch Bridge' and climbs away from Midford behind 9F No. 92220 'Evening Star'. The train comprised 12 coaches, weighing 426 tons, regarded as the heaviest load ever to be taken by a single locomotive over the Mendips – a record which belongs to my good friend Peter Smith who was in charge of 'Evening Star'.　　　　　　　　　　　　　　　　　　David Bartlett

Postscript...

Midford signalmen Percy Savage and Harry Wiltshire were determined that, despite the signs of outward neglect, the standards which they had always upheld would be maintained to the very end. Thus, the brass was polished, the floor was washed, the windows cleaned inside and out. And, when the door was locked after that final shift, the interior of Midford signalbox was as immaculate as it had always been.

Within days of closure the Western Region S&T engineers had stripped from the box all that was of value. What remained soon received the inevitable attention of vandals and the once-polished heads of the signal levers – already dulled – began to acquire a veneer of rust.

The up line from Wellow was retrieved first, the hills around Lower Twinhoe echoing to the throbbing engine of a BR diesel heading the track recovery train. Eventually the down line and the single line into Bath Junction were lifted and Mother Nature started to regain control of the strip of land she had lost nearly a century before.

During 1967 the station buildings had succumbed to demolition but the shell of the signalbox remained until... I know not when, for I had witnessed enough.

Signalmen Harry Wiltshire (left) and Percy Savage (right) pose together for the last time for the benefit of an old friend, Jack Pike, one-time stationmaster at Evercreech Junction.   Photo: the late W.A.J. Pike

Chapter Five

ALL ABOUT SIGNALLING

Details of the early signalling provided at Midford remain unclear. Before the doubling of the line to Wellow there were no sidings or points at Midford. Even so, a reference in the Board of Trade Report following the Foxcote accident of 7th August 1876, noted that Midford was provided with "two block instruments and a single-needle speaking instrument". These were positioned in the Booking Office and were, on the day of the accident, entrusted to the telegraph clerk, Edwin Hues, a 17 year old youth who worked, except on Sundays, from 7am to 9.55pm for a weekly wage of 5 shillings (25p).

Under the operating conditions agreed under Seal by the Directors of the S&D, only one train was permitted at a time in the section between Bath Single Line Junction and Wellow, the first crossing station. It would appear, however, that on occasions this undertaking may have been disregarded, with permission given for an up train to leave Wellow as soon as the preceding train had cleared Midford, and before its arrival at the junction at Bath. Such a practice appears to have been in operation on the night of the Foxcote accident and obviously some form of signalbox was in existence at Midford, for in November 1876 the Joint Committee approved plans to enlarge the signalbox "5 feet northwards, to allow the speaking telegraph instruments to be removed from the booking office", and also to provide the box with a stove. All this suggests that a small enclosed lever frame existed on, or near, the platform. In 1876 approval was sought for the interlocking of the signals to be removed "so that when the post is switched [out] they can be left at 'all right'." (Whether or not the Board of Trade approved the request is unrecorded!). References are also contained in the early Minute Books to the appointment, transfer and resignations of signalmen at Midford. Such activities appeared to be all too frequent, with men taken on, at a weekly wage of 18 shillings (90p), either resigning or soon moving on to more important duties.

BR class 9F 2-10-0, No. 92000 crosses Tucking Mill viaduct and climbs towards Combe Down tunnel with the 3.40 pm Bournemouth-Bristol Temple Meads on 31st August 1961. On the left is the Midford down distant signal.   Ivo Peters

The first publicly documented evidence of the signalling at Midford was the first edition of the Ordnance Survey map published in 1886, the area including Midford having been surveyed in 1884. This map indicated a total of four signalposts located as follows:

i). On the down side of the line at the foot of the embankment opposite Midford Park, just south of the cutting leading from Tucking Mill viaduct. (The unusual siting – at the foot of the embankment – may possibly have been to comply with one of the numerous Conditions agreed with the owners of the Midford Castle Estate.)

ii). On the top of the 'Long Arch Bridge' (in the same position as that occupied by the 'down home' signal in later years).

iii). On the station platform.

iv). On the down side near the southern end of the cutting south of Midford viaduct.

In January 1884 it was agreed that two starting signals should be installed, whilst towards the end of that same year, the Directors of the Joint Committee agreed that the new Railway Clearing House code of block signalling, as already adopted by the Midland Railway, should be introduced as soon as possible, the actual date of introduction being 1st March 1885.

Until 1886 the S&D was worked by the block telegraph, supplemented by the use of crossing orders. This was a system of working where the safety of the travelling public was totally dependent upon the strictest compliance with the Rules and Regulations. Human error could – and did – have tragic and terrible consequences, as witness the Foxcote accident of 1876. In 1886, however, the S&D introduced the use of the Tyer's train tablet system of working. The instruments were installed and brought into use between Bath, Wellow and Radstock on 3rd October 1886, and thereafter the train tablet system of control was to serve the S&D well for 80 years, until closure of the line in 1966.

From the date of the introduction of this new method of working, Midford obviously ceased to be a block post, as the Tyer's tablet instruments had been installed at Wellow and Bath Single Line Junction to control the block section between those points. However,

S&D 7F 2-8-0, No. 53810 heads a freight from Evercreech Junction towards the southern portal of the 'Long Arch Bridge', north of Midford Station. The down home signal was located high above the 'Long Arch'. The lower arm fixed to the same post was the 'repeater' for the 'wrong road' signal sited on the station platform. These distinctive 'wrong road' signals were often referred to, unofficially, as 'backing signals'.   Ivo Peters

Class 2P 4-4-0, No. 40697 and BR class 5, No. 73047 running past the Midford up starting signal with the 9.03 am Bristol Temple Meads-Bournemouth on 12th August 1961. On Thursdays only this train called at Midford to enable the staff wages, which were carried in a travelling safe, to be handed to the station master.

Ivo Peters

the signalbox and signals at Midford were retained and possibly worked only for trains stopping at Midford station, for a similar practice seems to have been in use at Spetisbury, south of Blandford. (Note, by the way, the reference to the 'Single Line Junction' box at Bath. Between 5th November 1876 and 13th April 1934 separate Midland Railway and S&D boxes existed at Bath Junction, replaced at the latter date by a single box.) An instruction printed in the S&D Appendix dated 1st February 1889 shows that a code of bell signals was in use between Wellow and Midford as follows:

WELLOW & MIDFORD
Instructions to be Observed as to the
Use of Bell Signals between Wellow and Midford

Bell Signals

To Call Attention	1 beat of the Bell
Down Passenger Train leaving Bath Single Line Junction	2 beats of the Bell
Up Passenger Train leaving Wellow, tickets not collected	4 beats of the Bell
Up Passenger Train leaving Wellow, tickets collected	4 pause 4 beats of the Bell

The Signalman at Wellow must send the Bell Signal to Midford for a Down Train, after having given permission for Bath Single Line Box to draw a Tablet, and for an Up Train on its leaving Wellow.

The "Call Attention" Signal must in all cases be sent and acknowledged by being repeated, before the distinguishing Bell Signal is forwarded.

Note the reference in this instruction to the collection of passenger tickets. The Midland station at Bath was, like many of its contemporaries, operated as an 'open station' and trains were halted before arrival to enable tickets to be collected. On the Midland line into Bath, Weston station served this purpose, but on the S&D extension a special 'Ticket Platform' was erected approximately ¾ mile south of the junction. The delays to traffic, however, soon persuaded the S&D to provide a replacement platform at Bath Junction, where a loop line could be laid in, thus allowing up trains to clear the single line before halting for the collection of tickets. This latter platform appears to have fallen out of use within a few years, with Wellow and Midford stations now assigned the task of ticket collection, at least for local trains.

New signal boxes were erected at both Wellow and Midford with the doubling of the line between these two places in 1892. The original tablet instrument for the Bath-Wellow section was transferred from Wellow to Midford signalbox and reconnected to control the shortened single line section into Bath. At the same date a ground frame was provided to control the new siding installed to the south of Midford viaduct. This ground frame, which later became known as 'Midford B', contained three levers, and was interlocked with the new signalbox.

BRITISH RAILWAYS – SOUTHERN REGION
MIDFORD GROUND FRAME "A".   No 192

SIDING

3 PUSH

3 PULL

FROM BATH

TO MIDFORD

← UP — DOWN →   2 1

[|||]
GROUND FRAME

F.P.L. STANDS NORMALLY "IN"

LEVER No:-	1	2	3 FULL	3 PUSH
DISTANCE IN YARDS	14.	14W.	15.	34.
FROM CENTRE OF BOX.	33.	31 E.		

MECHANICAL LOCKING

No	DESCRIPTION	RELEASED BY	WORK	LOCKING
1	F.P.L. & GATE LOCK.	TABLET	1	
2	SIDING POINTS	1	2	
3 PULL	SHUNT MAIN TO SIDING	1. 2.	3 PULL	
3 PUSH	SHUNT SIDING TO MAIN	1. 2.	3 PUSH	

Ex-GW Collett 0-6-0, No. 2219 returns light-engine to Templecombe, passing the Midford A Ground Frame, which controlled the entrance to the goods yard and was released by the Bath Junction-Midford single-line tablet.

D.W. Bartlett

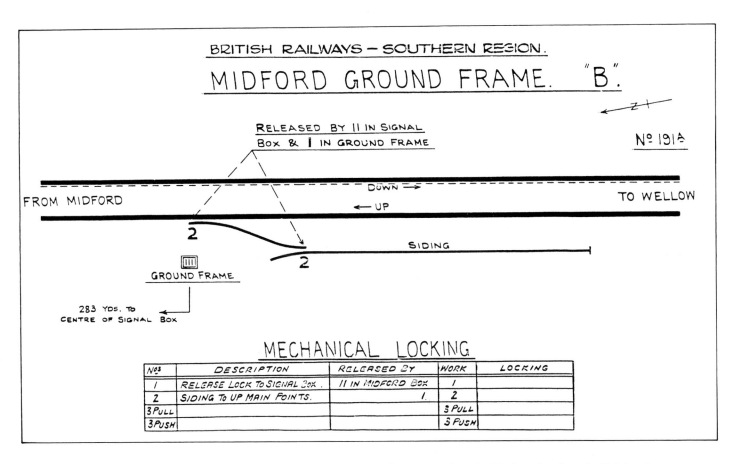

MIDFORD GROUND FRAME. "B".

Nº 191ᴬ

RELEASED BY 11 IN SIGNAL
BOX & 1 IN GROUND FRAME

FROM MIDFORD

DOWN →

← UP

TO WELLOW

2

2

SIDING

GROUND FRAME

283 YDS. TO
CENTRE OF SIGNAL BOX

MECHANICAL LOCKING

Nᵒ³	DESCRIPTION	RELEASED BY	WORK	LOCKING
1	RELEASE LOCK TO SIGNAL BOX.	11 IN MIDFORD BOX	1	
2	SIDING TO UP MAIN POINTS.	1.	2	
3 PULL			3 PULL	
3 PUSH			3 PUSH	

Midford B Ground Frame, controlling the connection to the up siding, is prominent in this view taken from the Twinhoe Lane on a sunny afternoon as class 2P, No. 40564 and rebuilt SR Pacific, No. 34028 'Eddystone' head south with a Bournemouth train on 29th August 1959.

Ivo Peters

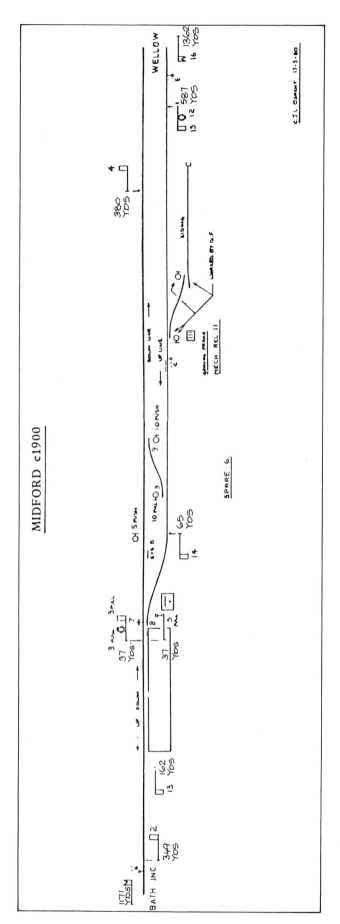

MIDFORD c1900

Whether the crossover road, between the up and down roads, was provided at this date remains unclear; but if not laid in during 1892 it was certainly installed within the following few years. The provision of the connection to the new goods yard in December 1894 was on the single line section and the new ground frame, later known as 'Midford A', was released by the Bath-Midford tablet. These works did not, therefore, directly affect the working of the signalbox.

In 1904 lineside apparatus was erected to allow for mechanical exchange of the single line tablets. The apparatus was patented by Alfred Whitaker, Locomotive Superintendent to the S&D. At Midford, the equipment consisted of a delivery standard placed immediately in front of the box on the up side of the line, and a receiver on the opposite (down) side. The provision of this equipment permitted considerable improvements to the services on the S&D, for the exchange of tablets could now be undertaken at speed.

By the early 1900s the layout and the extent of the signalling at Midford was as shown on the accompanying diagram, with the double-line section from Wellow extending right across the viaduct and the facing points positioned immediately north of the signalbox. The use of the crossover road is uncertain. Occasionally, at Midford, it was necessary to transfer wagons between the goods yard and the up siding, and the crossover would have permitted the engine to 'run round' the wagons before propelling them the short distance to the siding. A similar movement would be possible for the transfer of trucks in the reverse direction. Whatever the reason, however, the crossover, together with the controlling 'dummies' (ground signals), were removed during 1918, an S&D Officers' Minute dated April 1918 noting that:

Removal of cross-over road at Midford.	It was reported that the cross-over road between the up and down lines south of Midford station is not required. It was therefore agreed to recommend that it be taken out, that the original cost of the connection, namely £269 be credited to capital and debited to revenue and that the revenue be credited with the value of materials recovered, estimated at £95, less the costs of removal namely £86. The saving in maintenance will be about £4, and in renewals about £13 per annum.

Of the signalling which originated from the opening of the new box in 1892, all of the signal posts, other than No.5 Pull (of which more later), were of wooden construction; many were of considerable height and had all the appearance of Midland Railway origins, despite the fact that by this time the L&SWR had taken over responsibility for the signalling of the Joint Line. The

BR class 4 4-6-0, No. 75072 leaves the single-line section with a down train on 6th July 1959, and starts the 1 in 60 climb towards Wellow. On the left is the up inner home signal and, sited between the up and down tracks, the ground disc signal which enabled a train shunted onto the down line to return to the single-line as far north as the up starting signal.　　　R.C. Riley

Late afternoon, and the peace of the picturesque countryside around Lower Twinhoe is briefly disturbed as the 2.45 pm (SO) Bournemouth-Bristol Temple Meads, hauled by two BR 4-6-0s – class 5, No. 73019 and class 4, No. 75072 – passes the Midford up distant signal. The lineside embankment to the right was known to local railwaymen as the 'Spile Bank' but none could ever explain the origins of this name!　　　Ivo Peters

TYERS No 6. ELECTRIC TABLET APPARATUS.

Description of Tablet Apparatus (No. 6)—*continued*

The two instruments for the section are furnished with a number of train tablets. Only one of these tablets can be taken out of the instruments at any time, except when taken out by the Lineman as shown in Electric Token Block Regulations 23 and 31.

A tablet can be replaced in either instrument at any time without any communication being made with the opposite end of the section. The tablets for each block section controlled from any one signal box differ essentially, as do also the tablet instruments fixed in the box, so that a Signalman who has more than one set of tablets to deal with cannot by mistake place a tablet in the wrong instrument.

OUTLINE OF WORKING

"A" and "B" represent two stations.

"A" has a train ready to proceed towards "B".

"A" calls "B" as per code.

"B" replies as per code.

On receiving the last beat of acknowledgment **Is line clear** Signalman "A" will turn his commutator from right to left; the bottom disc then shows **out**. The Signalman must then withdraw slide containing tablet and give one beat on the bell-plunger, which will change the top disc at "B" from **In** to **Out**. "B" must acknowledge the bell signal.

On arrival of the train at "B" the Signalman will obtain the tablet, lift the lever at side of instrument, pull the slide out empty, place the tablet in the slide, lettered side downwards, push the slide home and give the prescribed signal **Train out of section**, which "A" must acknowledge.

"B" will then hold in his bell-plunger three seconds to enable "A" to turn his commutator from left to right and replace empty slide. "A" then gives one beat on bell-plunger which will turn the top disc at "B" from **Out** to **In**. "B" will then lift up lever at side of instrument, pull out his slide, empty, replace and give one beat which will change the bottom disc at "A" from **Out** to **In**. "A" must then give one beat, which "B" must acknowledge. The instruments are now normal.

NOTE.—The lever must not be lifted and empty slide withdrawn until top disc shows **Tablet in**. The Signalman must always be most careful to pull out and push home the slide to its full extent.

Cancelling No. 6 Instrument.—Replace tablet in slide, lift lever, pull out empty slide, replace and give cancelling signal to "B", which "B" must acknowledge by repeating.

Under no circumstances may an unauthorised person be allowed to operate the instruments.

ELECTRIC TABLET (No. 6)

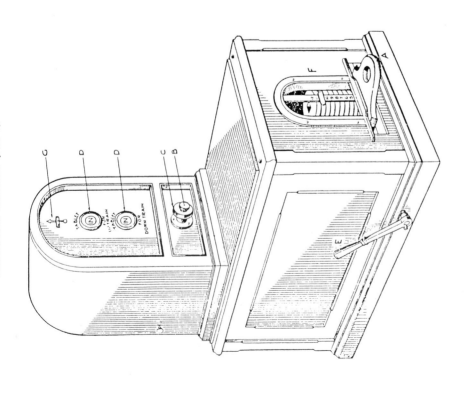

DESCRIPTION OF TABLET APPARATUS (No. 6)

The apparatus consists essentially of Slide "A", a bell-plunger "B", a Commutator "C", Disc signals "D", showing two positions "In" and "Out", a lever "E", a slot "F", and an indicator "G".

The slide "A" is for the purpose of withdrawing and inserting tablets.

The bell-plunger "B" serves to transmit all signals on the bells.

The Commutator "C" cannot be turned without the consent and co-operation of both Signalmen, except in connection with the **Cancelling** signal.

The Disc Signals "D" show whether tablet is **in** or **out**.

The lever "E" is for raising or lowering the Tablets in the cylinder and restoration of mechanical control to normal.

The Slot "F" shows the tablets in cylinder of apparatus.

The indicator "G" indicates all outgoing and incoming signals sent on the bell-plunger from either end.

Bells are supplied with each pair of instruments.

location of the 'Up Inner Home' signal (No.14) is of interest, the wooden post being secured to the side wall of the viaduct. Similarly, the 'Down Home' (No.2) was located, for ease of sighting by trainmen, on top of the 'Long Arch Bridge' and, as noted earlier, this site appears to have been used from the earliest days of the line's existence.

The tall post of the 'Down Starting' signal (No.3 Pull) originally sported a subsidiary arm (No.3 Push) which served as a shunt signal, authorising access onto the down line, presumably to enable movements to be made via the crossover road on the viaduct. It must have been taken out of use upon the removal of the crossover in 1918.

Early in 1912 it was reported that the train tablet apparatus in use between Bath and Midford was still the original (Tyer's No.1) pattern, and it was agreed to replace this with more modern apparatus (Tyer's No.6 pattern) at an estimated cost of £220. It will be recalled that the existing instruments were those originally installed between Bath and Wellow in 1886.

Perhaps the most intriguing and certainly the best known of Midford's signals was No.5 Pull; the arm fixed high upon a latticed post of L&SW origin and sited on the station platform. Officially known as a 'Wrong Road' signal, the arm was shaped like a bow tie. In June 1929 a repeating arm for this signal was provided and fixed, again for sighting purposes, on the same post as the 'Down Home' high above the 'Long Arch Bridge'. The use of these 'Wrong Road' signals enabled a train to be signalled from the single line back onto the up line. For example, the driver of a heavy northbound goods train occasionally found the steep gradients up to and through Combe Down tunnel somewhat daunting, usually as a result of a poorly steaming engine or a 'wet rail'. Rather than risk stalling in the tunnel, the driver would halt his train close to the tunnel mouth where, using a line-side telephone, he would inform the Midford signalman of

---

AUTOMATIC EXCHANGE APPARATUS—BETWEEN BATH JUNCTION, MIDFORD AND TEMPLECOMBE JUNCTION.

Apparatus is provided at stations and signal boxes on the single line sections between Bath, Green Park and Bournemouth West, also on the locomotives working over the line to enable the token to be exchanged automatically. With the exception of ballast trains, trains where the engine stops near the signal box and engines running tender first, when the token must be exchanged by hand, the apparatus must always be used and the token exchanged automatically.

Signalmen must ensure that the pouch containing the token is securely fastened, placed upright in the holder, and resting upon the lip at the bottom, also, in putting the arm in the working position, that the counterweight lever is close home to the stop. On Sundays and at other times when no staff are on duty, the arm must be secured by the padlock provided.

The ground apparatus will be maintained by the Signal Engineer's Dept. Defects must be reported by Western Region stations to the Bath Control Office and the Running and Maintenance Dept., Southern Region stations must advise the local Signal Inspector and the Trains Supervision Office, Southampton Central. If the defect is likely to render the apparatus inoperative for a lengthy period, the Motive Power Depot, Bournemouth should also be advised.

Passengers must not be allowed near the apparatus when it is fixed on or near the platform, neither must they be permitted to be near the platform edge when trains are passing through or arriving at the platform.

On locomotives, when a pouch is about to be given up, it must be placed in the holder after the distant signal has been passed. The exact time for this to be done must depend on the speed of the train, but it must be in sufficient time to ensure that the catcher is in its proper position well before reaching the ground apparatus. On engines fitted with the retractable catcher bar, the bar must not be pushed out until the engine is near the ground apparatus, and the handle should not be again touched until after the exchange has been made. The Fireman must always watch the exchange being made, using a handlamp during darkness to illuminate the engine apparatus. The pouch picked up by the engine must be examined by the Driver and placed in a safe position. The pouch must not be inserted in or removed from the apparatus while the engine is passing over a bridge.

In the event of a pouch being dropped or missed by the ground apparatus the Driver must stop the train immediately. All instances of failure to deliver or pick up the token must be reported by the Driver before leaving duty to enable the engine apparatus to be gauged by the Depot staff.

Pouches must be gauged by the Signalman on the gauge provided in the Signal Box. Any found to be defective in any way must not be used.

When it is not possible to provide an engine fitted with the apparatus, or should the engine apparatus be found defective, the Bath Control Office or the Train Supervision Office, Southampton Central, must be informed, to enable the Signal boxes concerned to be advised by telephone before the train leaves the starting point that the token will have to be exchanged by hand. The message will take the form of the code word "Pouch" followed by particulars of the train affected.

In 1951 Midford station and signalbox were still displaying the livery of the pre-nationalisation era – the green, cream and white of the former Southern Railway Company. The station also retained the original platform canopy which can be seen the distinctive 'wrong road' signal, which allowed a train to be shunted from the single-line back onto the up line beyond the southern end of the viaduct. In the foreground, the down starting signal has been cleared for the passage of a southbound train and the arm of the lineside automatic exchange apparatus has been extended ready to retrieve the pouch containing the single-line tablet. Immediately in front of the signalbox is the corresponding delivery apparatus, into which the pouch was placed and the arm rotated towards the track in preparation for the passage of an up train.

L&GRP, courtesy David and Charles

the situation. The signalman then sent the 'blocking back' bell code to Wellow box, and on receiving acknowledgement, would instruct the driver to reverse his train back down towards Midford, pulling off the 'Wrong Road' signals which authorised the driver to pass the down home and starting signals at danger. Halting at the box to return the single line tablet, the train could now be set back over the viaduct on the up line. Here, following a 'breather', the driver might decide to have another try, or alternatively, request that an assisting engine be sent out from Bath. If, meanwhile, there were any following up trains due, to avoid delay it would be necessary for the errant engine to draw its train forward again onto the single line and set back once more, this time onto the down line, an operation that required the single line tablet to be released and returned to the tablet machine once again!

The process of shunting an up train onto the down line at Midford to enable a following train to pass was, apparently, quite a common occurrence before the Second World War. That best known of S&D drivers, Donald Beale, has told how, in the 1920s, a late-running up freight train would be halted at Midford and set back onto the down line, to allow the up 'Pines' to pass. With the latter train clear, the driver of the freight might then have been instructed to draw his train forward once more and to reverse again back onto the up road to clear the down line for the passage of one or more southbound trains, before eventually 'getting the road' into Bath. In later years, however, this practice of shunting up trains at Midford virtually ceased, unless at the request of the driver who, on approaching Midford from the Wellow direction, had already decided he needed a 'blow-up' or the benefit of an assisting engine for the climb up through Combe Down tunnel. Otherwise an up freight would invariably be 'given the road' and, in the time-honoured manner, 'shown the duster' from the box, the signalman's way of telling the driver to 'Get a move on'!

The use of the 'Wrong Road' signals resulted in the need to provide special locking to the normal block working on the up line from Wellow, for it was essential that a backing movement did not conflict with any up train already accepted from Wellow. To provide this protection, the normal 3-position block instrument with Wellow box was interlocked with Sykes 'Lock and Block' instruments. To accept a train from Wellow, the Midford signalman had first to press a plunger on the Sykes instrument, the operation of which released an electric lock on the pegging handle of the normal block instrument, whilst at the same time locking lever '5 Pull' to prevent a conflicting movement. Once the Sykes instrument had been operated, it could not be plunged again until levers 13 and either 12 or 15 had been pulled and replaced; that is, until the train had gone into the forward section towards Bath Junction. Pulling lever 15

also caused the upper aperture on the Sykes instrument to show 'Locked' and No. 15 could not be pulled again until the train had passed over a track treadle (Treadle 'C' on the diagram), which released the back-lock. If subsequently a train had to return from the single line onto the up line (as in the circumstances already described), the working of lever No.5 Pull locked the Sykes instrument, thus preventing the acceptance of a train from Wellow. If all this sounds somewhat complicated – believe you me it was!

In 1923 the down line was track-circuited for a distance of 1000 yards south of the signalbox to assist the signalman in knowing when a down train had cleared the 1 in 60 gradient towards Wellow.

In 1933, the position of the facing point connection to the double line section was moved towards the southern end of the viaduct – 98 yards to the south of the box. This work was undertaken on Sunday 9th April 1933, and the repositioning of the points enabled the existing speed restriction of 20 mph in the up direction to be relaxed to 40 mph, a significant benefit not only to the heavy freight trains but in improved timing for through and semi-fast passenger traffic. The works also necessitated the resiting of the 'Up Inner Home' (No.14), the 'Down Advanced Starting' (No.4) and the ground signal (No.5 Push) controlling movements from the down to the single line. A new lattice bracket post was provided for No.14, which was now sited south of the viaduct, but the original tall wooden post was reused for No.4.

Subsequent replacement and resiting of other signals included the 'Down Distant' (No.1) and the 'Up Starter' (No.13) in 1942; the 'Up Outer Home' (No.15) and 'Calling On' signal (No.12), both affixed to the same post; and the 'Up Distant' (No.16).

As already related in Chapter Four, further and somewhat more dramatic alterations took place in 1936, as a result of the 'runaway train' episode. The post of the 'Down Starting' signal (No.3), "snapped off like a carrot" by the derailed trucks, is believed to have been rescued, and re-erected in cut-down form, nearer the signalbox, where it survived until 1961!

Other than the necessary reconstruction of the signalbox in 1936 and the sundry replacement of various signals, the layout at Midford remained unchanged from 1933 until the end of the 1950s. A fully annotated diagram of the signalling, together with locking details, is reproduced on pp 72-3.

In the mid-1950s a second track circuit was installed (track circuit 'B') reading through facing points 8 as far as signals 3, 5 Push, and 14, and replacing the original 'last vehicle treadle' (shown as 'L.V.T.B' on the 1950 diagram).

With the closure of the up siding towards the end of 1959, the 'Midford B' ground frame and the Calling On arm (No.12) were removed. WR influence became more apparent with the replacement of No.3 and No.4 signals

Signalman Percy Savage on duty in Midford box. This fine study, taken in 1955, shows the complete 16 lever frame, immaculate as ever. All levers, except Nos. 5 and 7, are standing 'normal' in the frame. No. 7, locking the single-line facing points, is 'reversed'. (Note, by the way, the duster without which no lever would be handled). No. 5 is a 'push-pull' lever and thus stands in mid-position. Lever Nos. 6, 9 and 10, painted white, are 'spares', i.e. unused. The dials fixed to the front of the block shelf are the signal lamp and arm repeaters; the plungers are electric lock releases to various levers. Left to the right on the block shelf can be seen the Midford-Wellow section block ball, the block instrument, a pair of track circuit indicators, and the Sykes 'lock and block' instruments.

Ivo Peters

in 1961. This saw the demise of the last of the original timber posts, the replacements coming in the form of standard WR tubular posts.

A much shorter replacement post for signal No.4 meant that the arm was no longer easily seen by the signalman. A lamp repeater was therefore provided in the box. Thereafter there were no further significant changes, although in the early 1960s a violent storm damaged the arm of the 'Up Inner Home' signal.

Over the years the original Stevens lever frame remained basically unchanged, retaining to the end the distinguishing square brass description plates attached to the signal levers.

Today, 20 years after the closure of Midford signalbox, the S&D Railway Trust has recreated some of the atmosphere of the old signalbox at their headquarters at Washford. Here, within the shell of the old GW (!) signalbox, a similar pattern frame, relocked to that which existed at Midford in the 1950s, has been installed, together with equipment identical to the original, including a Tyer's No.6 tablet instrument. Without doubt, the view from the Washford box will never vie with that enjoyed from Midford but at least 1987 should see an ex S&D engine (No.53808) finally restored by the Trust and passing the windows of the 'recreated' Midford box. Should you visit the West Somerset Railway, make sure that you stop off at Washford station, where, in addition to a fine S&D museum, you may, after a demonstration, be encouraged to try your own hand at working 'Midford' box!

Class 2P 4-4-0, No. 40698 piloting class 4F 0-6-0, No. 43875 'get the road', having been held at the up outer home signal, waiting for clearance of the Bath Junction-Midford single-line section which had been occupied by the down 'Pines Express'. Beneath the outer home arm is the 'calling-on' signal. The very tall down advanced starting signal can also be seen in the extreme left background.
Ivo Peters

MIDF

100 55
1196 YARDS

55 150
720

150 390
393

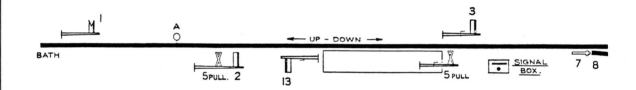

M¹   A
        O

3

← UP - DOWN →

BATH

5 PULL. 2   13   5 PULL   SIGNAL BOX.   7 8

MECHANICAL LOCKING

...ANCES	Nº	DESCRIPTION	RELEASED BY	WORK	LOCKING	WORK	TABLET OUT TO	SPECIA...
1171	1	DOWN DISTANT	4 3 2	1.				
357	2	DOWN HOME	7	2	12. 13			
10	3	DOWN STARTING	7	3	12. 13	3		
470	4	DOWN ADVANCED STARTING		4	5 PUSH			
35 357	5 PULL	SHUNT FROM PLATFORM TO UP LINE SIGNAL	8	5 PULL	12. 13. 14 (11 (11))	5 PULL		
206	5 PUSH	SHUNT FROM DOWN LINE DISC		5 PUSH	4 7. 8.	5 PUSH	BATH	
	6			6.				
51	7	F P L ON 8		7.	5 PUSH 8			
51	8	DOWN FACING POINTS		8.	5 PUSH 7			
	9			9.				
	10			10.				
	11	RELEASE LOCK TO GROUND FRAME	8.	11	12. 15	11		
668	12.	SHUNT BY UP OUTER HOME.		12	2. 3. 5 PULL. 11. 14.	12		
162	13	UP STARTING		13.	2. 3. 5 PULL	13	BATH	
206	14	UP INNER HOME.	8.	14	5 PULL. 12 (11 (11))	14	BATH	
668	15	UP OUTER HOME	14.	15.	11.	15		
1668	16.	UP DISTANT	13. 14. 15	16				
						UP PLUNGER		
						UP BLOCK COMM.		SYX INST.

ELEVATED FRAME.
CLOSING SWITCH :- NIL.
BLOCK TELEGRAPH TO WELLOW
Nº 6 TABLET TO BATH.

TRACK CIRCUIT INDICATED :- A.
ARMS REPEATED :- 1. 2. 4. (5 PULL REP.) 12. 15. 16.
LIGHTS REPEATED :- 1 (12. 15. 16)
ALL POINTS MECHANICALLY DETECTED.
ALL DISTANCES ARE IN YARDS FROM CENTRE OF SIGNAL BOX.

Nos. 12

TRACK

—SOUTHERN REGION

ORD

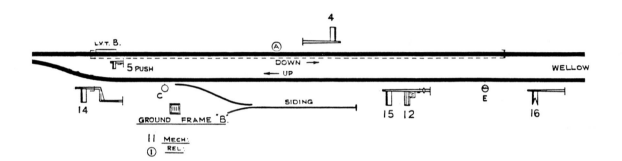

ELECTRICAL LOCKING & DETECTION.

NORMAL LOCK RELEASED BY			DETECTION		AFTER USE RELEASED BY	BACKLOCK RELEASED BY	LOCKS
TRACKS	TREADLE	LEVERS	MECH.	POINT BOLTS IN		TREADLE	
A			8	(7)		LV B	
			(8)	(7)		C	15 & UP PLUNGER TILL 13 P&R UP PLUNGER
							COMM: AT TABLET OUT TILL 3 OR 5 PULL OR 13 P&R
							15 & UP PLUNGER TILL 13 P&R. UP PLUNGER
						C.	15 & UP PLUNGER TILL 13 P&R
						A.	
							COMM: AT TABLET OUT TILL 3 OR 5 PULL OR 13 P&R
					13 P&R	C.	UP PLUNGER TILL 13 P&R.
					(12 OR 15) & 13 P&R.		5 PULL. 11 TILL 12 OR 15 P&R.
PLUNGED	E.	12. 15			12 OR 15 P&R		

OR 15 PULLED STOPS 'TRAIN WAITING' BUZZER & RESETS 'TRAIN WAITING' INDICATOR IN CONNECTION WITH TREADLE E.

CIRCUIT A 'OCCUPIED' OPERATES BUZZER.

Passenger... No. 40698 pulls away from Midford on 27th September 1952 with a Bath-Templecombe stopping train.

Ivo Peters

...and freight – a superb study of 7F No. 53806, one of the large-boilered series, running down through the cutting south of Tucking Mill viaduct with a down freight train on 23rd January 1954. The single-line section was re-sleepered about every 10 years and here the old sleepers have been laid aside for collection.

Ivo Peters

Chapter Six

PASSENGER & FREIGHT TRAFFIC

The S&D was developed primarily for heavy freight and through passenger traffic and over the years local passenger traffic was, invariably, the poor relation. A study of the S&D timetables reveals just how little the local services altered over the years and this can perhaps be best indicated by the following table which shows the trains serving Midford at various dates between 1876 and 1965.

Passenger Departures From Midford

Down Trains

Date	1876	1895	1910	1931	1950	1965
am	7.30	7.17	7.10	6.57	7.07	7.00
	10.30 (1)	9.17	9.05	8.42	8.27	8.27
pm	2.04	1.55	1.36	1.22	1.22	1.22
				3.05	3.22	3.32
		5.05	5.00	5.13	4.49	4.49
	6.23			6.47	6.17	6.17
	7.22	7.45	8.10	9.09	7.12	7.17
				11.12 (2)	10.14	10.38

Up Trains

Date	1876	1895	1910	1931	1950	1965
am	8.19	9.34 (3)	9.18	8.49	8.32	8.32
	11.08	11.10	11.21	10.54	10.50	10.37
pm				1.22	1.28	1.31
		2.40 (4)	2.54	3.31	4.05	4.12
	5.35	5.37	5.47	5.51	5.53	5.53
					7.45	7.53
	9.40	8.56	9.04	9.15	10.16 (5)	10.13 (5)

Notes:
1. Mixed train as far as Radstock.
2. Wednesdays and Saturdays only.
3. Depart 9.36 on Thursdays.
4. Midford stop introduced 1st July 1887 following local complaints about service into Bath.
5. Conditional stop to set down only.

The pattern of the service in the 1930s remained virtually unchanged for 35 years, and certain of the timings can be traced back to the service operated following the opening of the line in 1874!

In later years most trains primarily served as a means for short distance travel into Bath or, perhaps, to Radstock. In the summer months the 7.07am departure was the 'seaside special' for the locals, a slow train reaching Bournemouth West at 11.03am. The return from Bournemouth was timed to depart at 6.40pm, eventually pausing at Midford at 10.16pm, always providing the guard had been informed before reaching Radstock, for the Midford stop was 'conditional'! Weekday excursions were also regularly advertised to Glastonbury and Highbridge, travelling via Evercreech Junction on the 8.27am from Midford.

In the up direction the first train of the day, the 8.32am (7.00am Templecombe - Bath) served the needs of any office workers bound for Bath but was too late to be of use to the factory worker. Midford signalman Percy Savage would recall that when he first worked at Midford in the 1930s, this train (then timed slightly later at 8.49am) often conveyed loaded milk churns destined for a dairy at Bristol. One of the last local users of this service was a farmer at Twinhoe and Percy retained vivid memories of the horse-drawn cart slipping and sliding down the steep snow-covered lane, the driver a local worthy best remembered for always wearing his cap back to front! The heavy milk churns were unloaded onto the station platform, often just in time to meet the train.

The 10.50am and 1.28pm up departures were little used, although the latter train did provide a good connection at Bath with the 11.40am Bournemouth-Gloucester, which on Fridays was extended to Derby (not, I imagine, that many Midford people needed to travel to Derby!). The 5.53pm and the 7.45pm up departures enabled villagers to spend an evening out in Bath, returning on the last down train, the 10.00pm from Bath to Binegar, which halted at Midford for three minutes, the extended pause being necessary, not to dispose of any drunken revellers, but to enable the guard to extinguish the platform oil lamps!

Possibly the best patronised of the local trains was the 6.17pm down (6.06pm Bath-Binegar), the timing of which suited the homegoing commuter. Midford was, in later years, little used, unlike Wellow, which, devoid of any competing bus service, continued to be one of the best patronised stations on the northern end of the S&D.

Turning to the local freight traffic, Midford was shown in the Working Timetables for the 1890s as being served by up to four trains (2 up and 2 down). Invariably, however, the limited traffic needs of Midford could, in practice, be served by one daily service and this was reflected in the timetables from the mid-1920s. In addition to the traffic mentioned in earlier chapters, Midford yard was also regularly used by a firm of agricultural engineers based at Norton St. Philip for the dispatch of farm machinery. It was probably this same firm who, in later years, designed and built specialist railway wagons, including a viaduct inspection unit and a ballast cleaner. The company also designed some of the first winch and roller wagons for use of 'roll on/roll off' track laying. Much of the fabrication and welding work was undertaken in the goods yard at Midford, the Company building up the specialist vehicles on existing wagon chassis.

Radstock. Here the wagons would be detached and collected by the 6.05am Templecombe-Bath freight, eventually passing back through Midford around mid-day! Similarly, any inward traffic originating south of Midford would be taken by through freight to Bath, to be returned southwards to Midford by the 5.50am 'pick-up' the next morning.

No. 40568 and SR Pacific No. 34109 'Sir Trafford Leigh Mallory' run southwards through beautiful countryside between Midford and Wellow, with the 7.50 am (SO) Bradford-Bournemouth.
Ivo Peters

During the 1930s the yard was used for the occasional dispatch of walnut trees, purchased from local landowners and felled by a Bristol merchant for export via Tilbury. In the war years the goods yard was used for the transfer of explosives to temporary storage in an underground quarry at Upper Stoke. Whilst in early years the yard was frequently used by local farmers, the advent of the motor lorry ensured the loss of most of this traffic from the railway. By 1960 only the occasional load of sugar beet was received, for use as cattle feed, and invariably the 5.50am Bath-Evercreech 'pick-up' freight would steam straight past the goods yard at Midford. When, however, a call was necessary, any northbound traffic from Midford was first conveyed southwards to

Very occasionally one or more goods vehicles were transferred between the yard and the up siding to the south of Midford viaduct. To perform this move the driver of the 5.50am freight would halt his train on the 'Park Bank' on the down-grade north of the points giving access into the yard. After pinning down sufficient brakes the engine was uncoupled and ran forward in advance of the trailing points controlled from the adjacent Midford 'A' ground frame. The points were reversed, allowing the engine to enter the yard, collect the wagon to be trans-ferred and return to the main line. Now the points would be reset to normal, the wagon set back up the grade and the brake pinned down. The engine was now uncoupled and retired to the goods yard, whereupon the wagon was

An up local from Templecombe crosses Midford viaduct in 1955 behind 2P No. 40697. The driver and fireman watch to ensure that the single-line tablet is collected safely from the lineside standard in front of the signalbox.   Ivo Peters

'gravitated' down past the yard entrance points and once more brought to a halt. Finally the engine would emerge from the yard, couple up to the other end of the wagon and, with the 'wrong-road' signals pulled off, propel the wagon through the station and over the up line to the single siding south of the viaduct which was also controlled by a small ground frame (Midford 'B'), but unlike

the 'A' frame was mechanically interlocked with the signalbox.

In later years local freight at Midford was conspicuous by its absence but the same could not be said of through goods traffic which, during weekdays far outweighed passenger traffic over the northern end of the S&D, this being so until the second half of the 1950s.

Opposite page top: No. 40568 approaches with the 4.37 down local from Bath having cleared the single-line. But No. 53809 will still have to wait another 25 minutes until the 5.00 pm Bath-Evercreech freight passes before completing the journey into Bath. The driver, resigned to a lengthy delay, puts his feet up!
Ivo Peters

BR class 5 No. 73074 emerges from the 'Long Arch Bridge' on the approach to Midford station with a down train on 30th May 1955.

Ivo Peters

On a sunny evening in early May 1955 7F No. 53807 passes 'Midford B' ground frame and heads towards Bath. Note the leading bolster wagon conveying a large tree trunk, possibly bound for the sawmills next to the Midland goods yard at Bath.

Ivo Peters

Opposite page bottom: One of the fascinations of the S&D – the differing combinations of motive power. Elderly class 3F 0-6-0 No. 43436 assists a modern SR Pacific past 'Midford B' ground frame and up siding with the 7.45 am Bradford-Bournemouth on 11th July 1953.

Ivo Peters

The extent of this traffic can, perhaps, be best appreciated from the following table which provides details of typical weekday freight and passenger traffic passing through Midford in the mid-1950s:

Up	Down	
AM	AM	
	12Q05	11Q50 pm Bath-Evercreech freight.
	12Q45	12Q30 Bath-Evercreech freight.
1.54		10.45pm Templecombe-Bath freight.
2.24		9.28pm Poole-Bath freight.
	3.07	2.40 'Down Mail'.
3.09MX		1.40MX Evercreech-Bath freight.
	3.45	3.30 Bath-Evercreech freight.
4Q19		2Q50 Evercreech-Bath freight.
4.44MX		1.35MX Templecombe-Bath freight.
	5.15	5.00 Bath-Evercreech freight.
	6.05/20	5.50 Bath-Templecombe 'pick-up' freight.
	7.06/07	6.05 Bristol Temple Meads-Bournemouth West.
7.26/8.09		'Tablet out' from Bath Junction for daily working of Bath (Twerton) Co-op siding.
	8.26/27	8.15 Bath Green Park-Templecombe.
8.31/32		7.00 Templecombe-Bath Green Park.
	9.10	8.55 Bath-Evercreech freight.
	10.05	9.05 Bristol Temple Meads-Bournemouth West.
10.10		8.00 Evercreech-Bath freight.
10.48/49		6.50 Bournemouth West-Bath Green Park.
	11.35	11.20 Bath-Evercreech freight.
11.37MFO		9.30 Bournemouth West-Sheffield Midland. MFO.
11.47		9.45 Bournemouth West-Manchester Mayfield & Liverpool, Lime Street. (The Pines Express). (Conveyed Sheffield portion MFX)

PM	PM	
12.08		6.05 Templecombe-Bath freight.
	12.50	12.35 Bath-Evercreech freight.
	1.21/22	1.10 Bath Green Park-Templecombe.
1.27/28		12.00 Templecombe-Bath Green Park.
1.44		11.40 Bournemouth West-Bristol (extended during Summer only to Gloucester FX & Derby FO).
	2Q15	2Q00 Bath-Evercreech freight.
	3.03MFO	10.10 Sheffield Midland-Bournemouth West MFO.
	3.16	10.20 Manchester London Road-Bournemouth West (The Pines Express).
	3.26/27	3.15 Bath Green Park-Bournemouth West.
3.25X30		1.05 Evercreech-Bath freight.
4.12/13		12.55 Bournemouth West-Bristol Temple Meads.
	4.36	3.25 Gloucester-Bournemouth (3.30 from Bristol during Winter months).
	4.48/49	4.37 Bath Green Park-Templecombe.
	5.15	5.00 Bath-Evercreech freight.
5.35		3.20 Evercreech-Bath freight.
5.52/53		4.15 Templecombe-Bath Green Park.
	6.16/17	6.05 Bath Green Park-Binegar.
6.47		3.35 Bournemouth West-Bristol Temple Meads.
	7.16/17	6.02 Bristol Temple Meads-Bournemouth West.
	7.33	7.18 Bath-Templecombe freight.
7.27X38		5.00 Evercreech-Bath freight.
7.49/53		7.10 Binegar-Bath Green Park.
8.45		7.25 Evercreech-Bath freight.
	9.10	8.55 Bath-Evercreech freight.
9.48		8.25 Templecombe-Derby (perishables).
	10.11/14	10.00 Bath Green Park-Templecombe.
10D17		6.40 Bournemouth West-Bath Green Park.
	10.50	10.35 Bath-Templecome freight.
11.27		10.00 Evercreech-Bath freight.

Q	=	Runs when required.
X	=	Stops at Midford for 'line clear' only.
MX	=	Mondays excepted.
MFO	=	Mondays & Fridays only.
MFX	=	Mondays & Fridays excepted.
D	=	Sets down only.

But, of course, it was on summer Saturdays that the emphasis of traffic dramatically changed, with freight giving way to the through passenger trains between the North of England, the Midlands and Bournemouth.

In post-war years the vintage summer Saturdays were undoubtedly the mid-1950s but, ironically, when it came to variety of motive-power, it was perhaps as late as 1961 that the greatest number of differing classes and combinations of locomotives could be observed working over the line.

The 'classic' Saturdays were those immediately before and during the Bank Holiday periods when, in addition to the regular through traffic, several relief trains were run. These 'extras', together with corresponding empty coaching stock and light engine workings, ensured that on such Saturdays, the Bath Junction to Midford single line section was occupied to absolute capacity.

The general pattern of regular Saturday traffic over the S&D had become established over many years, with precedence being given to northbound traffic in the morning, and vice versa from the early afternoon. However, the running of relief trains often led to some retiming of certain regular traffic, in order to provide the necessary paths over the single line sections. The resulting schedules generally proved somewhat optimistic and, in practice, extremely difficult, if not impossible, to achieve.

The initial bout of activity at Midford centred on a group of overnight trains originating each Friday night from Sheffield, Derby, Bradford and Manchester. None of these trains were publicly advertised over the S&D but ran to regular timings each summer. On 23rd July 1955 – one of the busiest ever post-war Saturdays on the S&D – these regular workings were reinforced by three reliefs which, together with the regular down 'Mails', were booked to pass through the Bath Junction-Midford single line section as follows:

Train Reporting Number	Bath Jn. (passing times)	Midford (passing times)	Description
M 977	2.12	2.20	Birmingham-Bournemouth West relief.
341	2.37	2.45	10.00pm Sheffield (Midland)-Bournemouth West.
339	2.47	2.55	11.00pm Derby-Bournemouth West.
– –	2.59	3.05	2.40am Bath-Poole 'Mails'.
345	3.17	3.25	8.30pm Bradford Forster Square-Bournemouth West.
W 716	3.47	3.55	Coventry-Bournemouth West relief.
M 836	3.59	4.07	Derby-Bournemouth West relief.
132	4.12	4.20	10.39pm Manchester, London Road-Bournemouth West.

The other face of Midford! A class 7F 2-8-0 storms across the viaduct during the period in January 1963 when the S&D was overwhelmed by snow. The engine is running tender-first and working up as much speed as possible for the climb up to Combe Down tunnel.   Ivo Peters

2P No. 40568 and SR Pacific No. 34043 'Combe Martin' cross Midford viaduct on 13th September 1958 in charge of the up 'Pines Express'. The rails of the GW Camerton branch have recently been lifted and recovered but the sleepers still lie along the trackside. The tall chimney on the left belongs to the Hope and Anchor Inn.   Ivo Peters

Slotted into this procession of down trains was the 1.40am Evercreech-Bath up freight, whose arrival at Midford's up outer home signal at about 3.10am was made apparent by a 'repeater' in the signalbox, the indicator swinging over to show 'train waiting'. The treadle which operated this repeater also caused a buzzer to sound in the box to remind the signalman of the train's presence. This freight would be held waiting clearance of the single line section by the 8.30pm Bradford-Bournemouth at around 3.25am, when the freight would be given the road. Before long it would appear under a moonlit sky, the driver 'winding her up' to take full advantage of the short down grade before the adverse gradients up to and through Combe Down tunnel. The fireman would lean out over the cabside with his handlamp held to watch the collection of the single line pouch from the Whitaker apparatus directly in front of the signalbox. All being well, the goods would clear Bath Junction box at about 3.40am, following which 'Is line clear?' would be asked by the Junction signalman for the next down relief.

The only other freight which ran before late on Saturday night was the 1.35am Templecombe-Bath, passing Midford at about 4.45am. There would now be a

prolonged lull in activities, punctuated only perhaps by the occasional light engine returning to Bath.

At 5.00am the early turn signalman 'signed on', taking over from the night man. The 6.00am Bristol Temple Meads-Bournemouth West and the following 8.15am Bath-Templecombe stopping trains both called at Midford. On summer Saturdays both trains were invariably double-headed to Evercreech Junction in order to provide sufficient pilots for up expresses later in the morning. The first up local, the 7.00am from Templecombe, also paused at Midford station, the last train to do so for many hours.

On 23rd July 1955 the 8.20am Bristol-Bournemouth, hauled by No.44859, was booked to pass Midford at 9.15am, followed by a 10 coach relief from Birmingham headed by No.53802 and piloted by Class 4F No.44559, both ex-S&D engines. By now the time was approaching 10.00am, the hour that heralded the start of the busiest period. For the next five hours the average interval between one train clearing the Bath Junction-Midford single line section and a following train entering the same section would be just 4½ minutes. In several instances trains were timed to enter the section one minute after the preceeding train had cleared, a timing impossible to achieve in practice at Midford, even assuming that trains were running to time or in the correct order! The booked times for trains over the single line section on that day were as shown in the accompanying table. Needless to say things did not turn out quite as planned, and matters were not helped by a timing error contained in the Special Notice issued to cover the alterations and additional traffic that day. The 'Notices' had No.M988 up passing Midford three minutes before train No.241 down was timed to clear the single line section!

Although my details of motive power are, sadly, far from complete, it was evident that Bath shed was making full use of its latest acquisitions, the BR Standard Class 5's, whilst the engines they replaced, the Bulleid Light Pacifics, were being borrowed from Bournemouth Central in order to meet the very heavy traffic demands. Most piloting was in the hands of the '2P' 4-4-0s which gave such valiant service over the S&D. Note that Class 4F 0-6-0 No.44096 made two return journeys between Bath and Bournemouth, working in tandem with sister engine No.44556 on the 11.30pm Birmingham-Bournemouth

'Western' influence on the S&D. Ex-G.W. 0-6-0, No. 3210, and 7F 2-8-0, No. 53806, climb past the parklands of Midford Castle on 12th August 1961 with the 10.40 am (SO) Exmouth-Cleethorpes.
Ben Ashworth

Trains over Bath Jn-Midford single-line section.
10.00am to 3.00pm on 23 July 1955

Bath Jn (down) ———→
←——— (up) Midford

Reporting Number	Booked times			Description	Load	Train engine (and pilot) where noted
	9.57	——→	10.05	9.05am Bristol Temple Meads-Bournemouth West	6	BR '5' No.73074
M989	10.18	←—	10.05	8.00am Bournemouth West-Huncoat relief	10	'4F' No.44560 + No.44096
214	10.29	←—	10.19*22	8.16am Bournemouth West-Liverpool Lime Street	10	SR Pacific No.34095 + '2P' No.40509
213	10.34	——→	10.42	7.43am Birmingham New Street-Bournemouth West	8	'7F' No.53809 + '2P'
W711	10.49	——→	10.57	7.10am Walsall-Bournemouth West relief	12	'7F' No.53804 + '4F' No.44417
	11.07	←—	10.53*59	9.15am Templecombe-Bath Green Park		
228	11.17	←—	11.08	8.40am Bournemouth West-Bradford Forster Square	10	LMS '5' No.44830
234	11.39	←—	11.32	9.25am Bournemouth West-Liverpool Lime Street	12	BR '5' No.73073
236	11.54	←—	11.46	9.45am Bournemouth West-Manchester London Road 'Pines'	12	SR Pacific No.34043 + '2P' No.40563
M227	12.02	——→	12.10	9.15am Birmingham-Bournemouth West	10	SR Pacific No.34095 + '2P' No.40700
238	12.23	←—	12.09*15	9.55am Bournemouth West-Leeds City	9	BR '5' No.73050 + '2P' No.40527
225	12.26	——→	12.34	7.35am Nottingham Midland-Bournemouth West	10	BR '5' No.73051 + '4F'
246	12.43	←—	12.31*36	10.05am Bournemouth West-Cleethorpes	11	BR '5' No.73052 + ?
250	12.58	←—	12.51	10.35am Bournemouth West-Manchester Victoria	9	'7F' No.53808 + '2P' No.40698
W734	12.49*59	——→	1.07	9.15am Coventry-Bournemouth West relief	10	'4F' No.44096 + '2P' No.40601
	1.12	——→	1.21/22	1.10pm Bath Green Park-Templecombe stopping train		'2P' No.40509
	1.39	←—	1.30/31	12.03pm Templecombe-Bath Green Park stopping train		
254	1.47	←—	1.40	11.12am Bournemouth West-Derby Midland	9	SR Pacific No.34107 + ?
256	2.08	←—	1.55*2.00	11.40am Bournemouth West-Sheffield Midland	10	'4F' No.44557 + ?
241	2.19	——→	2.27	6.57am Cleethorpes-Bournemouth West (retimed)	9	BR '5' No.73073 + '2P' No.40568
M988	2.32	←—	2.22*24	12 noon Bournemouth West-Preston relief	8	LMS '5' No.44776
243	2.32	——→	2.40	9.40am Sheffield Midland-Bournemouth West	11	BR '5' No.73050 + '2P' No.40564
M264	2.52	←—	2.46	12.20pm Bournemouth West-Derby relief	10	'7F' No.53810
245	2.54	——→	3.02	7.50am Bradford Forster Square-Bournemouth West	10	SR Pacific No.34043 + '2P' No.40563

Note: *indicates held at Midford (up outer home signal) or at Bath Junction for Line Clear only.

and the 8.00am Bournemouth-Huncoat relief, and later heading the 9.15am Coventry-Bournemouth relief (loaded to 10 and unassisted south of Evercreech), finally to return with the 2.08pm Bournemouth-Wigston empty coaching stock – not a bad day's work for an elderly freight engine! Double return trips were also made by BR 5s Nos.73050 and 73073, the latter, together with No.73074, on loan to Bath from Patricroft for the summer season. It is also interesting to note the use being made of the S&D class 7F 2-8-0s, at least 6 of the class on passenger duties.

was now possible to see locomotives from many different companies – ex-Midland and LMS, Southern, BR Standards and even ex-GW. Was there any other line which provided the enthusiast with such a spectacle of motive-power?

Whilst the traffic intensity of the mid-1950s may have declined somewhat by the early 1960s, there were still occasions when the single line section was worked almost to capacity. The example of the Train Register book at Midford, on Saturday 29th July 1961, indicates one such day with five down relief trains and four return

S&D No. 53800 heads past milepost 4¼ on 25th July 1953 with a relief train from Walsall to Bournemouth. The engine is only yards from the point where the S&D joined with the former route of the coal canal tramway (see page 27).
Ivo Peters

Traffic normally quietened down in the late afternoon, but busy holiday weekends invariably resulted in the running of return trains of empty coaching stock to dispose of stock from unbalanced workings. Saturday 23rd July 1955 proved no exception, with the running of no less than 5 e.c.s. trains – the last passing Midford after midnight.

By the early 1960s the interest of the railside enthusiast was maintained by an even greater variety of motive-power, this offsetting the diminution in traffic. It

e.c.s. workings. Perhaps the most interesting event of that particular day was the use of 'Black Five' No.44771 (a visitor from Rugby) as pilot to No.53807 on the 9.55am Bath-Bournemouth West. Later in the day the engine returned to Bath piloting Bulleid Pacific No.34041 'Wilton'!

To anyone now visiting the site of Midford station it might seem almost impossible to believe that such traffic once used the line.

BRITISH RAILWAYS — Midford — Signal Box — DOWN LINE — Sat. 29th July 1961

Description how Signalled	Circuit Received	Rcvd but NOT Accepted	Acc. Reg 5	Acc. Reg 3	Train Entering Section Received	Number of Engine	Train Arrived	Train Departed or Passed	Train Out of Section, Signal Given	Offered but NOT Accepted	Acc. Reg 5	Acc. Reg 3	Train Entering Section Given	Train Out of Section, Signal Received	Time Given or Received	Obstruction Removed	Time Train ready to Depart	REMARKS
5.5.5				Recd. Wellow open 2.31													1	
1.3.1				2.44					2.59			2.49	2.58	3.2			2	
4				2.59					3.12			3.2	3.11	3.15			3	1080
4				3.17					3.37			3.25	3.36	3.41			4	1079
4				3.37					3.51			3.41	3.50	3.54			5	1082
4				3.55					4.9			4.0	4.8	4.12			6	1085
4				4.16					4.30			4.21	4.29	4.33			7	1084
				P. Savage off duty 5.0am				H. Wiltshire on duty 5.00									8	
3.1	6.48			6.54	7.02	7.10	7.11	7.12			7.02	7.11	7.18				9	
3.1	8.15			8.12	8.17	8.26	8.27	8.28			8.17	8.27	8.33				10	
4	9.27			10.0	10.06			10.14			10.06	10.13	10.18				11	1X42
3.1	9.55			10.14	10.17			10.25			10.18	10.24	10.29				12	
4	10.32			10.30	10.37			10.45				10.44	10.48				13	
4	11.15			11.18	11.20			11.29			11.20	11.28	11.33				14	1X71
4	12.00			12.00	12.02			12.11			12.02	12.10	12.15				15	1090
4	12.24			12.34	12.37			12.46			12.37	12.45	12.50				16	1091
				H. Wiltshire off duty 1.00				C Eyre on duty 1.00pm									17	
4				1.18	1.21			1.29			1.21	1.28	1.32				18	1X79
3.1				1.29	1.30		1.37	1.38	1.38		1.32	1.38	1.44				19	
4				2.24	2.28			2.37			2.28	2.36	2.40				20	1092
4				2.40	2.43			2.55			2.40	2.51	2.55				21	1093
4				3.03	3.06			3.15			3.06	3.14	3.23				22	1094
-				Boxer Light Engines Bath				T Combe 3.12									23	
2.3				3.21	3.30			3/			3.30	3/	3/				24	
2.2					3.30			4.0				37	44				25	
4				3.48	3.58			4.07			3.58	4.06	4.11				26	1095
4				4.28	4.32			4.41			4.32	4.40	4.45				27	1098
4				4.46	4.50			4.59			4.50	4.58	5.02				28	1097
3.1				4.59	5.02		5.09	5.10	5.11		5.02	5.10	5.15				29	
3.1				7.17	7.18		7.26	7.27	7.27		7.18	7.27	7.32				30	
4.1				8.18	8.19			8.30			8.19	8.29	8.31				31	
7.5.5				Received Wellow close 8.37 Reg 26 Radstock "B"													32	
				C Eyre off duty 9.00pm				P. Savage on duty 9.0pm									33	
3.1				10.28	10.31		10.41	10.42	10.42		10.31	10.42	11.04				34	

BRITISH RAILWAYS — Midford Signal Box — UP LINE — Sat 29th July 1961

Description how Signalled	Circuit Received	Rear: Recd but NOT Accepted	Rear: Accepted Reg 5	Rear: Accepted Reg 3	Rear: Train Entering Section Recd	Number of Engine	Train Arrived	Train Departed or Passed	Train Out of Section, Signal Given	Adv: Offered but NOT Accepted	Adv: Accepted Reg 5	Adv: Accepted Reg 3	Adv: Train Entering Section Given	Adv: Train Out of Section, Signal Recd	Block Back: Time Given/Recd	Block Back: Obstruction Removed	Time Train ready to Depart	REMARKS
4·1				12·18	12·41				12·59			12·41	12·59	19			1	
3·1	7.00			8·20	8·23		8·31	8·32	8·32			8·28	8·31	8·40			2	
Boxer Light Engine J'Combe–Bath @ 8·52																	3	
2·3	LE			9·08	9·18				9·23			9·18	9·23	10·00			4	
Boxer Light Engine J'Combe–Bath @ 9·31																	5	
3·1				10·35	10·44		10·50	10·51	10·51			10·45	10·50	10·59			6	
2·3	LE			10·51	10·51		10·55	10·59	11·00			10·59	11·00	11·08			7	
4				11·00	11·00		10·05		11·10			11·08	11·10	11·18			8	1N46
4				11·29	11·34				11·38			11·30	11·38	11·47			9	1M02
4				11·44	11·49				11·54			11·47	11·53	12·00			10	1M04
4				12·10	12·14				12·18			12·11	12·17	12·26			11	1N66
4				12·18	12·21		12·25		12·27			12·26	12·27	12·34			12	1M06
4				12·38	12·41		12·44		12·48			12·46	12·48	12·56			13	1M07
3·1				1·13	1·21		1·26	1·40	1·40			1·38	1·40	1·48			14	
Rule 55 by tel fireman JH 12.37 T Combe @ 1·30 pm																	15	
4				1·40	1·43		1·47		1·49			1·48	1·50	1·58			16	1E58
4				2·05	2·10				2·15			2·10	2·14	2·22			17	1E59
4				2·42	2·46		2·50		2·56			2·53	2·55	3·03			18	1M09
Rule 55 by tel Fireman JH 12.20 B smith @ 2·53 pm																	19	
3·1				4·05	4·11		4·16	4·17	4·18			4·11	4·17	4·25			20	
3·1				5·40	5·45		5·51	5·52	5·52			5·45	5·51	6·00			21	
2·2·1				5·52	5·53		5·57		6·02			6·00	6·01	6·10			22	3×46
4				6·58	7·05				7·09			7·00	7·08	7·17			23	
2·3	Bath			7·14	7·20		7·25		7·30			7·28	7·30	7·39			24	
2·2·1				8·00	8·06				8·11			8·00	8·11	8·19			25	3×47
4				9·11	9·33							9·33	9·43	9·51			26	
3·1				10·02	10·03		10·19	10·20	10·20			10·03	10·19	10·28			27	
2·2·1				11·37	11·49				12·00			11·49	11·59	12·07			28	3×48
Sunday 30th July																		
2·2·1				12·58	1·05				1·16			1·05	1·15	1·23			29	3×49

TRAIN REGISTER – EXPLANATORY NOTES

Each line of the Register has been numbered (see the column headed 'Time Train is ready to Depart'). The references below are numbered to correspond to the appropriate entry in the Register.

Down Trains

1   Wellow signal box opening signal received at 2.31 am.
2   2.40am Bath Green Park-Poole (Down 'Mail').
3   10.00pm FO (Fridays Only) Sheffield-Bournemouth West retimed. (Running 15 minutes late).
4   11.00pm FO Derby-Bournemouth West (retimed). (20 late).
5   8.25pm FO. Bradford-Bournemouth West. (26 late).
6   12.15am Coventry-Bournemouth West relief. (13 late).
7   10.28pm FO Manchester Victoria-Bournemouth West. (17 late).
8   Duty change. Signalman Harry Wiltshire on 'early turn'.
9   5.58am Bristol Temple Meads-Bournemouth West. (15 late).
10 8.15am Bath Green Park-Templecombe. (2 late).
11 6.45am Birmingham-Bournemouth West relief.
12 9.03am Bristol Temple Meads-Bournemouth West. (19 late).
13 7.43am SO Birmingham New Street-Bournemouth West. (2 late).
14 7.15am Walsall-Bournemouth West relief.
15 9.08am SO Birmingham-Bournemouth West (which actually started at Nottingham at 7.28am).
16 7.35am Nottingham-Bournemouth West relief. (11 late).
17 Duty change. Signalman Charlie Eyre on 'late turn'.
18 9.10am Coventry-Bournemouth West relief. (16 late).
19 1.10pm Bath Green Park-Templecombe stopping train.
20 7.00am SO Cleethorpes-Exmouth. (14 late).
21 9.35am SO Sheffield-Bournemouth West. (11 late).
22 7.43am SO Bradford-Bournemouth West. (12 late).
23 Boxer (box-to-box message) at 3.12pm advising light engines running Bath to Templecombe loco.
24/25 Light engines. (2 coupled).
26 10.30am SO Manchester-Bournemouth West ('Pines'). (26 late).
27 10.20am SO Liverpool-Bournemouth West Relief. (9 late).
28 10.55am SO Manchester-Bournemouth West. (28 late).
29 4.35pm Bath Green Park-Templecombe stopping train. (21 late).
30 6.08pm SO Bristol Temple Meads-Bournemouth West stopping train. (13 late).
31 Bath-Templecombe freight.
32 Wellow signalbox closing signal received at 8.37pm.
33 Change of duty. Signalman Percy Savage on 'night turn'.
34 10.25pm Bath Green Park-Templecombe stopping train.

Up Trains

1   Evercreech Junc.-Bath freight.
2   7.00am Templecombe-Bath Green Park stopping train.
3   Boxer message at 8.52am advising light engine running from Templecombe-Bath.
4   Light engine to Bath loco.
5   Boxer message at 9.31am advising light engine Templecombe-Bath.
6   7.12am Bournemouth West-Bath Green Park. (2 late).
7   Light engine to Bath loco.
8   8.40am SO Bournemouth West-Bradford.
9   9.25am SO Bournemouth West-Crewe*. (2 late).
10 9.45am SO Bournemouth West-Manchester ('Pines'). (6 late).
11 9.55am SO Bournemouth West-Leeds. (8 late).
12 10.05am SO Bournemouth West-Derby. (Held at Midford 'up outer home' signal (No. 15)).
13 10.32am SO Bournemouth West-Manchester (Held at No. 15).
14 12.03pm SO Templecombe-Bath Green Park stopping train. (Held at No. 15).
15 Rule 55 by telephone by fireman of 12.03pm Templecombe detained at No. 15.
16 11.12am SO Bournemouth West-Sheffield. (Held at No. 15).
17 10.40am SO Exmouth-Cleethorpes. (19 late).
18 12.20pm SO Bournemouth West-Nottingham. (Held at No. 15).
19 Rule 55 by telephone by fireman of 12.20pm Bournemouth held at No. 15.
20 1.10pm Bournemouth West-Bristol Temple Meads stopping train (5 late).
21 4.14pm Templecombe-Bath Green Park stopping train. (2 late).
22 Empty coaching stock ex. Bournemouth West.
23 3.40pm Bournemouth West-Bristol Temple Meads.
24 Light engine from Templecombe-Bath loco. (Held at No. 15).
25 Empty coaching stock ex. Bournemouth West.
26 7.27pm SO Bournemouth West-Bristol Temple Meads.
27 6.48pm Bournemouth West-Bath Green Park stopping train.
28 Empty coaching stock ex. Bournemouth West.
29 Empty coaching stock ex. Bournemouth West.

*Crewe was the destination given in the 1962 WR Working Time Table, but this train ran through to Manchester and Liverpool, as in previous years.

Note: The times shown in the column headed 'Circuit Received' are departure times ex. Bath Green Park.

2P No. 40697 and 7F No. 53810 climb the 'Park Bank' northwards from Midford with an up express on 4th August 1951. The lineside observer is Mr. O.S. Nock. The GW branch running towards Monkton Combe can be seen in the background (to the left of the pilot engine's exhaust).

Ivo Peters

7F No. 53808 raises the echoes as she climbs towards Twinhoe Bridge with the 11 am down goods on 15th January 1963. In the background station master Keith Cooper can be seen struggling back to Midford, having gone out and checked the up distant signal – a round trip of 2 miles, not to be envied in such adverse conditions.   Ivo Peters

---

Instructions to Enginemen and Guards respecting the Working of Freight Trains Worked by Nos. 4 and 7 Class Engines

Down Trains

Enginemen
Bath and Midford.
On the train emerging from Combe Down tunnel the driver should apply sufficient steam to keep the couplings well strained. On passing Midford signal box the regulator should be opened as necessary and not eased until the train has reached the level at the top of Midford bank.

Guards
Bath and Midford.
Gradually apply brake after whole of train has entered Combe Down tunnel, increasing, as necessary, to take strain of couplings. On emerging from tunnel, continue to hold same until van is passing Midford signal box, when brake must be eased, and finally released as van passes the up inner home signal.

Up Trains

Guards
Midford.
Guards should apply handbrake gradually when passing up distant signal to take strain of couplings and release when passing Midford signal box.

(From the S&DJR Appendix to the Working Time Tables dated 1933.)

No. 53809 and SR Pacific No. 34103 'Calstock' cross Midford Viaduct with the 12.20 pm (SO) Bournemouth-Nottingham on 1st September 1962, passing over the abandoned GW line. Just 3½ years later the S&D would suffer the same fate. On a happier note, ex-S&D 7F No. 53809, was to be spared the breaker's torch and, restored to running order, can now be seen at Butterley, the headquarters of the Midland Railway Trust near Derby. Sister engine No. 53808, owned by the S&DR Trust, should also return to steam in 1987 to run between Minehead and Bishop's Lydeard on the West Somerset Railway.

B. Ashworth

Chapter Seven

MEMORIES OF MIDFORD

On reflection, I suppose that it all started as the result of a birthday present and a lion. The birthday present was a new bicycle and the 'Lion' was the historic Liverpool & Manchester Railway locomotive, resurrected from a museum to star in a comedy film to be entitled 'The Titfield Thunderbolt'! News had spread through the loco-spotters' grapevine that the 'Lion' had arrived at Westbury loco depot, but by the time I had persuaded my father to take me to the sheds, the 'Lion' had already been steamed successfully, and departed to a branch line south of Bath, where Ealing Studios were shooting scenes for the new film.

Undeterred by this setback and fired by enthusiasm to try out my new steed, I persuaded my parents to allow me to set out one summer afternoon with the intention of hunting down the 'Lion'. Seven weary miles distant, most of which seemed to have been uphill, found me entering the village of Hinton Charterhouse. By this stage the initial enthusiasm had waned to the point where I seriously considered giving up the hunt and returning home. However, a visit to the village shop revealed that my quarry might be found just 2 miles away and more important, it was downhill all the way! Armed with this information and reinvigorated by half the contents of a bottle of 'Tizer' (the loco-spotter's favourite drink!), I set forth with renewed enthusiasm.

Freewheeling down the long hill, the warm summer breeze carried the sound of a distant train – and across the valley a plume of smoke betrayed the passage of a freight train plodding slowly southwards through the Somerset countryside. Halting briefly, I struggled in vain to identify the motive-power at the head of the train. Strange, for at an early age, I had prided myself on being able readily to identify most classes of ex-GW engines. But the monster here seen in the distance was something new and, for the time being, a mystery it would remain, as the train had now disappeared from view.

Another half-mile and I reached the bottom of the hill, where lay the cottages of a small hamlet. Beyond, on the other side of the valley, the village was dominated by a long, high brick viaduct but on entering the village I passed under a much lower, iron-girdered railway bridge. Now as the roadway curved and started to climb, the viaduct came into view again, looking even more impressive at close hand. Passing under the viaduct, I found, beyond a pair of cottages, a lane leading off to the right; at the far end of this lane, a small railway station. Placing my bicycle against the timber paled fence, I passed through an open gate leading to the platform

ramp and a single set of railway lines. Immediately to the right, a signalbox, the occupant of which had already observed my arrival as he stood at the open window facing the end of the platform. "Excuse me", I ventured, "is this where the 'Titfield Thunderbolt' is being filmed?" "Not here", came the immediate reply, "you want the 'Western'", and pointing down to a rusty set of rails in the valley below the station, added "no doubt they'll be over at Monkton Combe today".

Well, I was going no farther and anyway there was something strangely fascinating about this little station. For a start, the buildings were not painted in the familiar 'Western' colours to which I was accustomed. Then there were the signals: they too appeared different, especially the one sited along the platform, a lofty latticed post with an arm that resembled an 'X', all extremely intriguing to the young enquiring mind. Finally, there was the matter of that unidentified engine, still, as yet, unsolved.

I retired to the platform bench seat, from which there was a panoramic view of the beautiful countryside. I remember that afternoon as though it were yesterday: the little station bathed in sunshine; the single platform with its wooden buildings, apparently deserted apart from my own presence. I stayed perhaps, little more than an hour, yet within that brief period I witnessed the passage of three trains; the first headed by a locomotive still bearing the initials 'L.M.S.' on her tender; the second, a Bulleid light Pacific and, finally, a large 2-8-0 freight engine and therein lay the answer to that unidentified engine seen from a distance earlier in the afternoon, for this engine, No.53808, appeared to be identical.

On that July afternoon I had, quite by accident, discovered and become immediately enchanted by the S&D. The station was Midford and over the ensuing 13 years, no matter how many times I returned, the excitement of that first afternoon never waned.

On my very next visit I met the Midford stationmaster, Mr Ryan, and decided it would be prudent to seek his official approval for me to use 'his' station bench for no better reason than 'to watch the trains go by'. Permission was duly granted, providing I behaved myself and "kept out of the way of passengers". What passengers I mused, for in my first two visits, I had yet to see one!

My first foray along the platform revealed that, immediately beyond the main station building, stood a small parcels store and beyond again, a handgate which gave access to a seemingly endless steep flight of steps leading up to the stationmaster's house and the narrow lane high above the station. I later discovered that, at times the parcels office had doubled as a Gentlemen's hairdressers and the steeply sloping hillside behind the station was a well-known source of excellent pea and bean sticking. All involved the intricate art of barter that abounded on the S&D. So, whilst the porter cut the hair, a train might be seen leaving the station with a bundle of bean sticks on top of the coal tender or in the guard's van!

Even farther along the platform, beyond the station nameboard, was a lean-to store which served as the lamp room. But it was towards the southern end of the platform to which I was inevitably drawn, towards that inviting flight of steps which led up into the signalbox. On that very first visit I had spoken to the signalman from the end of the station platform. Each subsequent opportunity to exchange small talk with the signalman found me venturing slightly further from the platform – ever closer to the box! Eventually I had reached the bottom of the signalbox steps, albeit fearing that I would soon be sternly ordered back to the nearby platform. But no, I was allowed to stay put and, as a result, conversations with the signalman became more frequent. No doubt he had seen it all before as he watched me from his open window gazing up at him, willing him to invite me up! Then one day, after many visits, those magic words: "Oh come on then; up you come if you want to!"

Percy Savage works the night turn.   The late Peter Girdlestone

Dear old Percy Savage, did he really know what he was letting himself in for? For that day proved the first of countless visits over the next 13 years and, until shortly before his death in 1982, he still welcomed me to his home to reminisce about the good old days. Percy's colleagues were Harry Wiltshire, another very kind and 'dyed in the wool' S&D man, and Charlie Eyre, a north-countryman who hailed from Chesterfield. It was perhaps Charlie who, over the years, taught me most about the art of signalling. He also taught me other skills, not the least 'adder catching'. For the sunny railway cuttings around Midford proved a favourite haunt of adders and Charlie took delight in suggesting we catch one. This we achieved with the aid of the signalbox coal tongs and poker: "I'll grab its tail with the tongs Mike, and you pin its head down with the poker", an operation that used to frighten the living daylights out of me (and no doubt the snake) and Charlie knew it!

Class 4F No. 44272 running light to Bath was not fitted with a tablet catcher. Signalman Charlie Eyre holds up a 'big pouch' for the fireman to take by hand.   M.J. Arlett

But I digress, for the main interest was not in snake catching but in what lay behind the entrance door to the signalbox. That very first visit into the box was just ten minutes in duration but was long enough to take in much of the detail, although to be honest, at that time I was unaware of the function of much of the shining equipment I saw. But in time, thanks to the patience of my tutors, I learnt a great deal of the workings of the box, although, of course, only very occasionally was I permitted the opportunity to try my own hand.

Inside the box, in the front corner, stood the Tyer's No.6 tablet instrument, controlling the single line section between Midford and Bath Junction. A tablet, when released, was inserted into a leather pouch, a supply of which hung on a row of hooks below the window. Across the front of the box, the sixteen lever frame was surmounted by the block shelf with an array of block instruments, bells, electric locks, track circuit indicators, lamp and signal arm repeaters, all polished to perfection. Above, and suspended from the flat roof timbers, was the signalbox diagram, whilst to the rear of the frame the signal wire compensators, the use of which enabled the wires controlling the more distant signals to be adjusted to compensate for the expansion and contraction caused by temperature changes. Across the far side of the box, a row of lockers which contained everything from detonators and 'Wrong Line Orders' to old copies of the 'Horse & Hounds', the last supplied by Charlie Eyre to be laid down to protect the polished linoleum floor on rainy days, such was the pride taken in maintaining the interior of the box. Woe betide anybody who entered without first wiping his shoes on the doormat provided! On, or against the rear painted brick wall of the box: the telephone instruments; the stove, regularly 'blacked and polished' and complete with kettle; the 'Weekly Notices'; and the train register desk, above which ticked the clock. Finally the signalman's chair, an ancient rocking chair held together at its base with twine, which had long prevented any rocking action, but none the less comfortable for that!

One of Midford's signals deserving special mention is the up distant, not that it was in any way unusual, but because of the years that passed before I finally succeeded in properly pulling off the signal arm! The up distant was located just 92 yards short of a mile from the box and the connecting wire from the lever in the box to the signal arm followed the tortuous route of the railway south of Midford, which abounded in reverse curves. Considerable effort was therefore required to pull off the signal. The art was to pull over the lever in one continuous action. I, however, could only succeed in pulling the lever part way, having to pause before giving another, final, heave. A glance at the signal arm repeater only to see the needle on the dial steadfastly pointing to 'Wrong' – try again! "Charlie: this signal wire needs adjusting".

"Nothing wrong with the signal wire, Mike, only the fool that's pulling it!" And to prove his point, Charlie grabs the duster, returns the lever to its normal position, pulls it over again and points to the repeater, now showing that the signal is 'Off'!

I also experienced problems at the other end of the frame, trying to overcome the complexities of the Tyer's tablet instrument. To release a tablet, the standard bell codes were first exchanged and, on receiving the last beat of the acknowledgement, the commutator on the instrument had to be turned anti-clockwise. The commutator, however, could only be turned if a foot contact on the floor of the signalbox was simultaneously depressed. Try as I might, more often than not I failed to co-ordinate the necessary hand and foot movements, a failure which heralded an immediate response from the Bath Junction signalman, via the telephone: "What the hell's going on?" "It's all right Fred, we've got a Learner here today" and, hanging the phone back on the hook, a somewhat exasperated tutor would ask, "Can't you do anything right?"

These occasional lessons in the finer arts of signalling were given during a quiet spell, usually on a weekday evening. Summer Saturdays were, of course, an entirely different matter, when it was prudent not to push one's luck and to retire to the station seat. Whether an invitation to "come on up" was offered depended on a variety of circumstances, not the least being the receipt of a 'boxer' (a telephone message sent from box to box) warning that 'higher authority' was about, and was heading this way!

But even from the platform, the working of the box could be seen and heard and I never ceased to be impressed by the almost casual way in which the signalmen dealt with the heavy traffic, which on occasions was running to a sequence which bore little resemblance to the 'Working Book'. Only occasionally did it appear necessary to contact 'Control' at Bath. "I've got the Walsall relief waiting – do I give her the road, or hold her?" "No", comes the reply, "get the damn thing out of the way as soon as the down clears – we want the locos here as soon as possible". Boxer messages were frequently exchanged and enquiries via the omnibus line inevitably evoked some mild abuse or sarcastic comment from a colleague listening in farther down the line. "I don't know why you flap so much, you've only got one bloody line to worry about at Midford. You want to come down here and find out what it's all about!" "Is that you....? Get off the line. If you spent less time listening to other people's business and more time learning the 'Rules', you might get promoted to a proper [signal] box one day. Now, where's the 'Pines' got to?" "I wouldn't worry too much about the 'Pines' yet Charlie, she's only just 'on line' here". And so it went on!

On 5th September 1959 4F No. 44523 and 7F No. 53801 lift the 9.08 am (SO) Birmingham-Bournemouth up the 1 in 60 climb southwards from Midford viaduct past the tall and impressive 'down advanced starting' signal.
R.C. Riley

On those summer Saturdays prior to and during Bank Holidays, many extra trains were run and on such days 'Special Notices' were prepared and issued detailing the running times of the reliefs and any necessary retiming or other alterations to the traffic. The crossings at Bath Junction and Midford – and on the single line sections south of Templecombe – were carefully worked out, by "bloody fools in offices", as Charlie used to say, with an allowance of one minute between the clearance of a down train at Midford and 'train entering section' for an up train. In practice this was a timing impossible to achieve at Midford where the following sequence of events had to be completed. First the signalman gave the Train Entering Section signal to Wellow for the down train clearing the single line section. Then down the signalbox steps and across the line to retrieve the pouch containing the single line tablet from the lineside apparatus. Back up to the box and, if not already done, return the down signals to danger before placing the tablet into the instrument and 'knocking out' to Bath. Immediately ask Bath Junction 'Is Line Clear?' for the up train and withdraw a tablet. Release the facing point lock and pull over the points to set for the up road. Now pull off the up starter, inner home and outer home signals. The up train which had been held at the last named signal, some 668 yards distant, would now be heard setting off down the 1 in 60 grade, during which time

the single line tablet would be inserted into its leather pouch, taken down the signalbox steps and placed into the lineside standard. The standard would be swung out for the pouch to be collected by the catcher on the train engine, which by now would be approaching over the viaduct... One minute's work indeed! Many was the time I watched the signals being pulled off; I would hear the train approaching and wonder if Percy Savage would manage to put the tablet out in time. Of course he always did, for that seemingly casual approach, to which I have already referred, was in reality a demonstration of the expert way in which all of the men went about their duties.

Sometimes traffic was so heavy that even those responsible for scheduling the extra traffic seemed in doubt as how to fit yet another train into the pattern of up and down trains over the single line. On more than one occasion the 'Special Notices' included a timing against which the letter 'B' would appear – and at the bottom of the page the reference 'B – crossing to be arranged' which, in reality, meant 'work it out as best you can on the day!'

Stories about the single line tablet were legend, but a few, at least, were true. It was known, for example, that during the war a relief signalman at Midford forgot to put the tablet into the pouch before inserting the latter into the lineside standard. Shortly after a heavy up freight

94

train had passed the box, the fireman came 'on the phone', using the special lineside telephone provided near the entrance to Combe Down tunnel. The conversation is reputed to have gone somewhat as follows. Fireman:- "We haven't got the tab". Signalman:- "Of course you have, I watched the exchange from the box." Fireman:- "Oh we got the pouch all right, but there's no bloody tablet in it!" Panic ensued within the box until the signalman's gaze fell upon the tablet machine. There, still lying on top, was the single line tablet. Back to the phone "It's OK, I've still got it here". Fireman:- "It might be 'OK' for you chum, but we've got to reverse back down and collect it". The comments of the train crew, on reaching the box, are unrecorded! In this instance there was, of course, no danger, as the tablet had been properly drawn from the machine and both instruments remained locked until the tablet was inserted into the machine at Bath Junc., or returned to the machine at Midford.

Generally speaking the exchange apparatus for the single line tablets proved extremely reliable but at Midford 'misses' did sometimes occur. Up trains seemed to fare worse, for during my own visits I can only recall two or three misses with the lineside catcher on the down side. The usual cause of a 'miss' was traced to misalignment of the catcher on the locomotive. The margin for error was small and if, for example, the locomotive

rolled at the vital moment the jaws of the catcher would strike the pouch and hurl it at considerable speed through the air. On such occasions Midford platform was not the safest place to be standing! Hopefully the pouch would come to land where it could readily be found, usually up against the station building. I always marvelled at the reactions of the train crews, who would succeed in bringing their train to an unscheduled halt usually before the locomotive passed far beyond the other end of the platform. Whether those passengers partaking of their lunch in the restaurant car saw it in the same light is a matter for conjecture! If the pouch had come to rest against the station wall it was hastily collected and there was a sprint along the platform to meet the fireman, who had dismounted from the footplate and was running back to collect the tablet. In what seemed no time at all the train was away again. But those few minutes – and the extra time now required to lift the heavy train up the grades to Combe Down tunnel from a 'standing start' could play havoc with the timetables and cause repercussions for many hours. How much worse then, on those rare occasions when the tablet, instead of coming to rest where it could readily be found, disappeared from sight. As the search became more frantic, the continuing delay would bring enquiring heads to the windows of the carriages. Eventually, the stationmaster would make the decision to introduce pilotman working

2P No. 40696 pilots 'Black Five' No. 44917 across Tucking Mill viaduct with the 10.30 am (SO) Liverpool, Lime Street-Bournemouth in the sunshine of a late afternoon on 2nd July 1955.   Ivo Peters

until the tablet could be found, or as was more often the case, the linesman was called out and the instrument adjusted to enable ordinary working to be resumed. However, before the linesman undertook this duty, he required the assurance of the stationmaster that a full search had been conducted and that the original tablet could not be found.

Sometimes the exchange of tablets would be by hand, either because the engine was not fitted with the usual exchange apparatus, or for some reason the apparatus was defective. For such occasions, a supply of 'large pouches' were kept at Bath Junction and Midford signalboxes. Inevitably pouches and tablets tended to accumulate at one or other end of the single line section. Tablets were transferred by the linesman under special regulations and the number of tablets transferred was recorded in the linesman's register and in the train register book. Pouches were, however, returned tied together. I recall one afternoon when the signalman at Bath Junction rang through to Midford box to advise that he was sending back some pouches with a pair of light engines working back to Templecombe after piloting up trains earlier in the day. Some eight to ten minutes later, the two engines appeared into view, the fireman of the second engine leaning over the cabside with the hoops of the pouches held out for the signalman to catch. Any reader who has experience of catching a single pouch will appreciate why signalman Charlie Eyre thought better than to chance his arm (literally!) in catching four such pouches tied together. Shouting to the fireman, whose engine had by now passed the signalbox, to 'throw them to the ground' the fireman duly obliged, but not until the engines were half way across the viaduct, thus ensuring a short walk to retrieve the pouches, one of which of course contained the single line tablet!

It was very rare for a down express to be halted at Midford, but on one occasion driver Donald Beale with fireman Peter Smith were returning southwards with the 'Pines' and on approaching Midford, Donald noticed that the 'down home' signal, sited high above the 'Long Arch Bridge' was standing 'on'. It became apparent to Donald that the crew of the pilot engine had failed to notice the signal. No doubt they had never been stopped here before. Donald therefore made an emergency application of the brake and brought the train to a halt within the confines of the 'Long Arch' and things were getting decidedly unpleasant. For although only 37 yards long, the clearance was minimal and, with the engine blowing off and making much black smoke, the effect was much the same as getting stuck within Combe Down tunnel! Donald therefore quickly reversed his engine, pushing the train back up the grade and pulling the pilot engine, the driver and fireman of which must have been wondering what on earth was happening until the whole ensemble was clear of the 'Long Arch'. By this time, the down starter had been cleared, so off they set again! Peter Smith related this story to me when we were filming together recently for the BBC, but Peter could not recall why the signal was at danger. Possibly the Midford signalman was experiencing problems with the lineside tablet catcher, or maybe he wished to pass a warning to the locomotive crew; perhaps animals had been reported on the line somewhere between Midford and Wellow. But as Peter said to me "The last place I expected to get nearly suffocated was the 'Long Arch' at Midford!"

At the north end of Midford platform, south of the 'Long Arch', Charlie Eyre always kept a watchful eye on the passage of 'down' trains. Perhaps it was an uneven rail joint or the curvature of the line which would sometimes cause an engine to roll, and the combination of a well-stocked tender and the lurching movement of the engine would occasionally cause a spillage of coal, whereupon, following clearance of the train, Charlie would point to a large old wicker basket in the corner of the box. "Right Mike, off we go" and we'd trudge up the line, carrying the wicker basket between us, to collect the 'free' coal used to supplement the signalbox supply; at least, Charlie always made out that it was destined for the signalbox stove – surely he didn't cart it all the way home to Wellow!

But if that particular source of 'free' coal was possibly put to official use another was certainly not. There was one nocturnal freight train from which 'fell' choice lumps of coal with almost monotonous regularity in the vicinity of Midford. The fuel, it was strongly rumoured, was destined for one of the local hostelries, but trade came to an abrupt end when, one night, the guard misjudged his whereabouts and a very large lump of coal heaved from the verandah of his brakevan, reduced the door of a linesman's hut to kindling wood. The evidence was hastily removed – and extensive enquiries by Management drew a blank – but painted firewood, whilst found to burn very well, tended to create an unacceptable amount of black smoke!

In the Spring of 1958 electric light finally reached Midford signalbox and the stationmaster's office (but not the remainder of the station) and the old Tilley lamps were discarded. No doubt they would be collector's items today. By 1960 I had acquired my first car and at last the one major deterrent to my visiting Midford (for the cycle ride home had commenced with two seemingly endless miles of steep hillclimbing) was finally overcome. The benefit of a car permitted more frequent nocturnal visits to the box and, perhaps more relevant, when Charlie was on 'late turn' we could get away from the box shortly after 9pm, race through the narrow lanes of Twinhoe and reach the New Inn (today the Fox & Badger) at Wellow well before closing-time for a pint of Indian Pale Ale!

Towards the end of 1960 stationmaster Bob Ryan moved on to take charge of Midsomer Norton station (and the ex-GW station at Welton) farther down the line. He was replaced, in January 1961, by Keith Cooper who was to prove the last stationmaster at Midford, for in 1964, the station was reduced in status to that of an unstaffed halt. In the interim Mr Cooper witnessed the blizzard conditions of January 1963, which had been preceded the previous September, by the withdrawal of the through passenger traffic between the North, the Midlands and Bournemouth. The period beyond the end of the Summer service of 1962 were unhappy days for the line and all those who served it. Time was running out for the S&D.

I will conclude my own memories on a happier note, a recollection which involved my wife who, in the days before our marriage, sometimes 'allowed' me to revisit the signalbox and indeed occasionally accompanied me on an evening trip. One such night we had been sitting in the box for more than an hour talking to Charlie Eyre and, no doubt, drinking his tea when Sandra began to display all the signs of wishing to spend a penny. "Charlie – I think Sandra wants to visit the Ladies' ". "Oh, go and see Keith Cooper, he's got the key to the door." She walked, no, she ran along the platform and knocked on the Stationmaster's door. "Mr Cooper, could you unlock the door to the Ladies' please?" Yes, he would, but on turning the key in the lock announced "You'll have to hang on a little longer my dear" and disappeared through the door. After what must have seemed an eternity to Sandra he reappeared, brandishing a large piece of cloth. "I had to dust the seat, it's not been used for ages." What a service they used to provide on the dear old S&D!

Midford Station 1966...

...1986

Above: M.J. Arlett   Below: Mac Hawkins

MIDFORD MEN

'Pen-pictures' and personal reminiscences of some of the S&D personalities that I have had the pleasure of knowing.

Charles Eyre (Signalman)

During the years in which I regularly visited Midford, Charlie Eyre probably suffered me more than any other S&D man and many of the happy memories I still retain are a direct result of Charlie's friendship.

Charlie Eyre hails from Chesterfield, and reached 'the Dorset' via Lawley Street and other signalboxes in the Birmingham area. Following spells of duty at Wellow and at Weston (Bath), he transferred to Midford box. In 1964, when the decision was made to close the S&D at night, Midford became a 'two-turn' box and Charlie transferred to Limpley Stoke box on the ex-GW line between Bathampton and Bradford on Avon.

Today, I still have the pleasure of occasionally bumping into Charlie in his local at Hinton Charterhouse.

Right: Charlie Eyre puts out the tablet for the up 'Pines'.

M.J. Arlett

Courtesy Mrs. W. Wiltshire

Harry Wiltshire (Signalman)

Harry Wiltshire began his working life on the S&D at Highbridge Wharf, where he recorded the wagon numbers of all out-going freight traffic from the busy wharfside lines. In 1924, he moved to nearby Bason Bridge, where he was employed as a porter. Two years later, in January 1926, he transferred to Wellow, still on station porter duties.

During 1940 Harry transferred to Wellow signalbox, being 'passed out' as a signalman later that year. In 1943 he applied for and was selected to fill a vacancy at nearby Midford box but after only a short period found himself back on portering duties as 'relief' covering many of the S&D stations. Early in February 1945 however, Harry returned to take up his post again as signalman at Midford, this time to remain for 21 years until the closure of the line. The closure of the S&D was a bitter blow to Harry who, like many of his S&D colleagues, had given a lifetime of service to the line.

There will be many a railway enthusiast who will always retain happy memories of a visit to Midford signalbox, thanks to the kindness of Harry Wiltshire. Like Percy Savage, he took the greatest pride in his work. Harry died on 7th November 1981.

Percy Savage (Signalman)

Percy Savage joined the S&D in 1920 as a 'Lad Porter' at Masbury. Some of Percy's earliest recollections were of the weekly trek down the line to Winsor Hill to attend to the signal lamps, a pleasant enough task on a warm Summer day but an altogether different matter in the depths of Winter! In 1922 Percy was transferred to Henstridge, where, he recalled, some of his time was spent assisting with the cattle traffic shunted into the single siding at that small station.

In 1930 another move took Percy to Midford as a porter where his duties included working in the (then) busy goods yard. The next move was to take Percy far away from the S&D – to Bidford-on-Avon, about 6 miles west of Stratford-on-Avon, on the old Stratford-on-Avon & Midland Junction Railway, which ran from Broom Junction to Blisworth.

Following a term of duty at Bridgwater (the S&D station of course!), Percy found himself back on the S&MJ line this time at Ettington, 5 miles east of Stratford. Returning yet again to the S&D, Percy worked at Sturminster Newton, Shepton Mallet and Burnham until, in 1935, he successfully applied for a vacancy at Highbridge Loco signalbox.

Finally, in June 1937, Percy transferred to Midford box, a post he was to hold for nearly 29 years until closure of the line in 1966.

On a personal note, Percy was the first S&D man I met, when in the 1950s he invited me into Midford box, for what was to prove to be the first of countless visits. Following his retirement, I continued to visit Percy and his wife where, nearly 30 years after our first meeting, he was still as prepared as ever to answer my various queries and to talk about 'the good old days' at Midford.

Percy Savage was a kind man who always took an immense pride in his work. He died on 3rd September 1982. I was proud to have known him as a friend.

Possibly the finest, and certainly the best known, picture of an S&D signalman. Percy Savage on duty in Midford box.   Ivo Peters

Bob Ryan (Station Master)

The start of Bob Ryan's career on the S&D was at Bridgwater in the early 1920s. During the Second World War Bob saw active service in Sicily and North Africa, before finishing up in Italy.

On returning to railway duties after the war he spent some time at Glastonbury station before moving to Cole as Station Master. He moved to Midford in the late 1940s, where he was responsible for both Midford and Wellow stations. During his stay at Midford he witnessed the nationalisation of the railway and the subsequent 'takeover' of the S&D by the Western Region of the newly-formed British Railways.

Bob finished at Midford in early November 1960, transferring to the station house at Welton, where he took up the responsibility of both Welton and Midsomer Norton South stations.

After the closure of the S&D he completed his time on 'filling-in' duties at various locations, including Westbury and Bath Spa. Bob retired from service on 28th February 1969.

Jack Watton (Porter)
The advertising board displays the heading panel 'Somerset & Dorset Joint Railway' but close observation of the advertisement extolling the virtues of Paignton reveals that the railways have been nationalised.

Both photographs courtesy Mrs. M. Ryan

Keith Cooper (Station Master)
Regrettably I have no full picture of Keith

Bob Ryan was succeeded as station master at Midford by Keith Cooper, who moved into the station house and took up his duties in January 1961. Keith started work on the railway at Kingsbridge as a booking clerk in March 1953. He also saw duties at Brent and Gara Bridge before moving to Midford.

Keith was to be the last station master at Midford for, in 1963, the station was reduced in status to that of 'unstaffed halt'. Keith then took up relief station master duties on the S&D line until, in mid-1964, he moved to Bristol Temple Meads as a relief inspector. Further moves saw him at Bristol East Depot as yard inspector, at Acton as relief area yard manager and again at Bristol as divisional traffic inspector. After a period at Westbury as Instructor at the Training Centre, today he acts in a similar capacity at Waterloo.

Keith still lives in the old station master's house at Midford.

Jack Taylor and Gang 180

'Gang 180' was the Midford permanent way gang, whose 'length' of line extended from the junction of the S&D and Midland lines at Bath to 'milepost 5' situated beyond Twinhoe Bridge in the Wellow valley. In charge of the gang from 1956 was Sidney George Taylor (but known always as 'Jack' Taylor), who had started work on the S&D at Evercreech Junction Station in 1914 at a weekly wage of 10 shillings (50p). He was, however, tempted onto the land by a local farmer offering 15 shillings (75p)! Jack next moved to join the labour force at the local brickworks, but business was hit by the recession. Facing redundancy, he was taken on again by the S&D, but initially only on a temporary basis, joining a group engaged in laying down the 'New Yard' at Evercreech Junction. (These were the sidings on the down side of the branch line to Highbridge). The temporary employment was extended, with Jack assigned to the Relaying Gang. In the mid-1920s he was transferred, as a permanent member of the Gang, to Wellow where he still lives in retirement. Other members of Gang 180 in later years included Albee Reardon, Ern Withers, Ces Marsh, Ted Elkins, Percy Smith, Chris Burdon and Andy Andrews. Despite the difficulties and dangers of both Combe Down and Devonshire tunnels, the gang won the award for the highest standard of permanent way maintenance in the Bristol District on more than one occasion, the last being in 1961.

BRITISH RAILWAYS
WESTERN REGION

THIS IS TO CERTIFY THAT

SIDNEY GEORGE TAYLOR
WAS GANGER OF GANG 180 WHICH

WAS AWARDED THE PRIZE FOR HIGH STANDARD OF PERMANENT WAY MAINTENANCE ON THE CLASS 'B' LINES OF THE

BRISTOL

DISTRICT IN 1961

DISTRICT ENGINEER   CHIEF CIVIL ENGINEER

'Gang 180' with Motor Trolley No. B29W. Both the trolley and the trailer were housed in the lean-to sheds immediately south of the signalbox. The gentleman to the left in the trilby hat is 'Jack' Taylor.   Photo Col. E.A. Trotman

Ivo Peters

Long before I started work on this book I decided that I would want to pay special thanks to a very kind friend, Ivo Peters. To this end, I make no apology for including Ivo under the chapter heading of 'Midford Men', for although Ivo retains such fond memories of the S&D in its entirety, I know that, like me, he has always held a special affection for Midford and the splendid isolation of the picturesque Midford and Wellow valleys.

So many tributes have been written to Ivo's superb pictorial record of the S&D, so richly enhanced by his ability to write such informative captions to his photographs that perhaps the best compliment I can pay is that, thanks to Ivo, more enthusiasts today can claim an intimate knowledge of the S&D than any other railway line in the British Isles. Indeed, there can be no other person who, single-handed, has so popularised, dare I say immortalised, any English railway.

For my part, I have enjoyed the pleasure and privilege of Ivo's friendship for some years, a friendship which has made the writing of this book far easier than might otherwise have proved the case. For many has been the time when Ivo's photographs have served to jog the memory sufficiently to recall some half-forgotten detail. Over recent years I have had the pleasure of seeing many times Ivo's superb 16mm colour films of the S&D. Now these films are available to the general public and, thanks to Ivo's foresight, it is possible to relive even more vividly memories of the old line.*

Despite a very serious illness, Ivo has offered me every assistance in preparing this book, including the encouragement to select freely unpublished photographs from his collection.

Above: 2P No. 40568 and SR Pacific No. 34044 'Woolacombe' burst out of Combe Down tunnel into the sunshine of Horsecombe Vale with the 7.50 am (SO) Bradford-Bournemouth on 21st August 1954. The fireman of the leading engine has spotted Ivo, who was unaware that....

Left:....in turn, he was about to be captured on film!! The fireman leans out of his cab to acknowledge Ivo who, of course, was well known to many of the S&D enginemen.

The late Peter Girdlestone

*Ivo Peters' Somerset & Dorset Railway
Vol. One – Bath-Masbury
Vol. Two – Masbury-Broadstone
Videos by Railscene Ltd.

MIDFORD STATION

Midford station was unique amongst those built on the 'Bath Extension' in that the construction of the main building was of timber. It has been suggested that this form of construction pre-supposed rebuilding if and when the line between Bath Junction and Midford was doubled. A prominent feature of the original station, which survived until 1953, was the canopy with its deep decorative valancing.

The main building measured some 60 feet in length and about 8′ 4″ in width and housed from left to right (i.e. south to north) as viewed from the platform: the 'Gents' (access to which was via the doorway in the end elevation), the 'Ladies' Room'; a storeroom, the door to which was marked 'Private'; the 'Ticket Office & Waiting Room'; and finally the Station Master's Office. The timber cladding consisted of horizontal lap boarding with rebated joints, the structure resting on a brick plinth which was visible only at the south end where the platform ramp sloped down to meet the access path. Doors were either four or six-panelled, all with small glazed transoms over. The two small upper panels in the door serving the Ladies' Room were also glazed.

Windows were double-hung sashes. Note the timber board nailed across the lower sash to the left of the Waiting Room doorway. This was to prevent the window pane being smashed by the projecting wrought-iron end support to the bench seat sited on the platform immediately in front of the window! Notice also the wide moulded architraves to both the window and door openings, and the positioning of the various advertising and timetable boards. The heights of some of these boards were altered in 1953 by the removal of the 'heading panels' on which appeared in painted lettering L.M.&S.R., SOUTHERN, etc. whilst at least one board still displayed the initials S.&D.J.R.! The station clock was sited between the doorway and window to the Station Master's Office.

The rear wall, also of timber, was hidden from view by the hillside into which the station was built. There was, in fact, a brick retaining wall immediately behind the rear wall of the building.

The flat roof was pitched at about 8 degrees and covered with corrugated asbestos-cement sheeting. The roof projected forward approx. 5′ 3″ from the front of the building to form the canopy which extended the full length of the building. As already noted, the main feature of this canopy was the boarded valance which was some 30″ from top to bottom. Regrettably, in 1953, the 'Western' saw fit to remove this feature, the existing roof timbers being cut back to provide only an 18″ overhang and finished with a plain timber fascia board. This totally altered – and destroyed – the appearance of the original building, which thereafter always looked somewhat 'mean', although on the plus side it was now possible to take advantage of the sunshine when watching the trains go by! Of the original valance, only that portion affixed to the south return end of the station building remained. Until at least the mid-1920s the valancing was painted in the alternative light and dark colours often seen on S&D station canopies in earlier years.

This enlargement of the view reproduced on page 68 shows the station building little changed from the 1880s. Soon, however, the platform canopy would be swept away and the Southern Railway livery replaced by the chocolate and cream of BR(WR). The poster boards still display the names or initials of the pre-nationalised railway companies and the station seat and 3-wheeled trolley are both survivors of a much earlier era.   L&GRP courtesy David & Charles

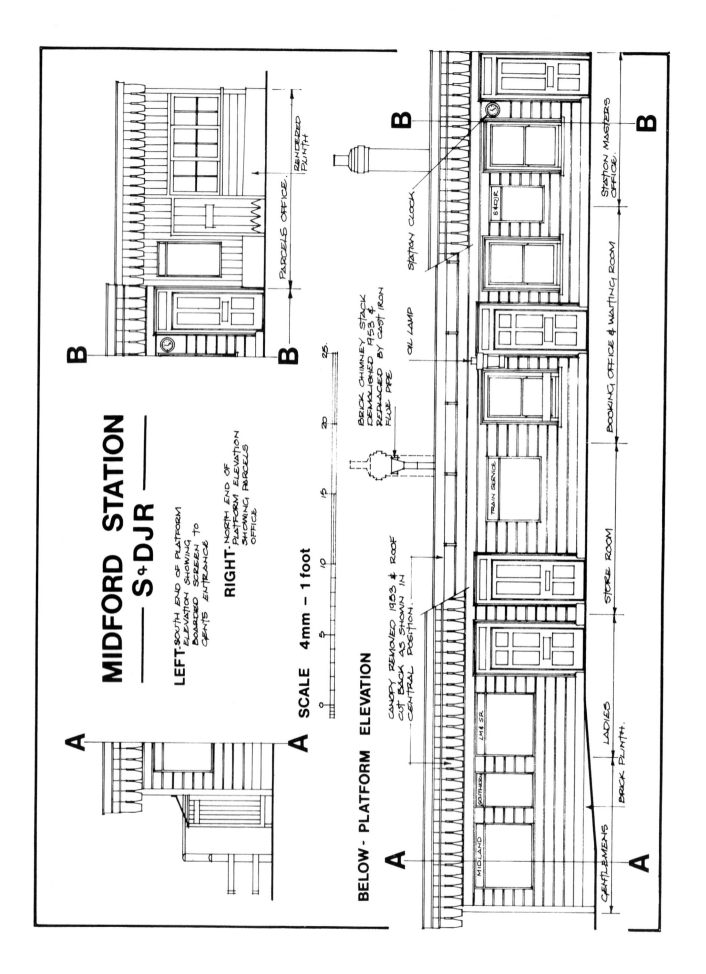

MIDFORD STATION
— S&DJR —

LEFT- SOUTH END OF PLATFORM ELEVATION SHOWING BOARDED SCREEN TO GENTS ENTRANCE

RIGHT- NORTH END OF PLATFORM ELEVATION SHOWING PARCELS OFFICE

SCALE 4mm – 1 foot

0 5 10 15 20 25

BELOW - PLATFORM ELEVATION

PARCELS OFFICE.

RENDERED PLINTH

BRICK CHIMNEY STACK DEMOLISHED 1953 & REPLACED BY CAST IRON FLUE PIPE

OIL LAMP

STATION CLOCK

CANOPY REMOVED 1953 & ROOF CUT BACK AS SHOWN IN CENTRAL POSITION.

STATION MASTERS OFFICE.

BOOKING OFFICE & WAITING ROOM

STORE ROOM

LADIES

GENTLEMENS

BRICK PLINTH.

TRAIN SERVICE

MIDLAND   SOUTHERN   LM & SR

S&DJR

The 18″ square brick chimney stack serving the Station Master's office was of considerable height – no doubt to counter the inevitable 'down-draughts' caused by the overshadowing hillside and trees at the rear. Before 1953 there was a second 18″ square brick stack serving the Waiting Room. This stack was slightly shorter and, when demolished, was replaced by a 4″ diameter metal flue pipe onto the top of which was fitted a wrapper plate to keep out the rain.

At the south end, the access to the Gents' was bounded by a high concrete block wall (possibly erected when the new access to the station was built in 1894). Victorian morality demanded the open doorway to be masked from the platform by the provision of a vertical boarded screen affixed to and extending back at 45 degrees from the front corner of the building. The small rectangular plate fixed to the end wall immediately below the valance was a sign warning of the fragile asbestos roof sheeting and advised on the need to use 'crawling boards'.

The two horizontal rails at the rear of the platform at the south end of the building were removable to permit loading and unloading of light goods, large parcels and, in pre-motor vehicle days, milk churns.

In addition to the main building, a Parcels Office was provided at the north end abutting the Station Master's office. It is uncertain whether this structure was a part of the original facilities or, as suspected, a later addition, for the joinery details differed from those of the main building. The overall size of this building was some 13′ 10″ x 8′ 4″, again of timber construction, but built on a rendered plinth. There was also a brick separating wall and a weighing machine inside. The building projected forward 3′ 9″ beyond the frontage of the main building, and was only 5′ 11″ from the platform edge. The timber windows were divided by glazing bars (other than the small window facing south). Horizontal boarding was affixed to the front elevation below sill level and on the south side. All other boarding was vertical. The roof, again, was of asbestos but to a steeper pitch than the main roof. Note how the lower edge of the valance boarding was cut off to a horizontal line adjacent to the rear corner (above the three fire buckets).

Immediately to the left of the doorway to the Waiting Room was the only external (oil) lamp fixed to the station structure although there were additional lights fixed to cast-iron lamp standards (one sited inside the access gate, another on the steps leading up to the lane above the station, one at the top of the same steps, one at the foot of the access road and two further along the platform).

Towards the north end of the platform a lean-to building acted as the Oil Store and Lamproom. The station platform was finished in tarmac with a brick edging and was 9′ 4″ wide measured from the main Stores doorway.

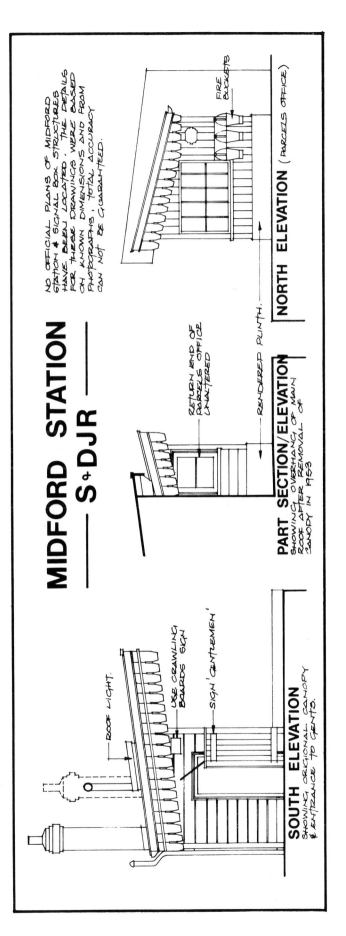

MIDFORD STATION
— S&DJR —

NO OFFICIAL PLANS OF MIDFORD STATION & SIGNAL BOX STRUCTURES HAVE BEEN LOCATED. THE DETAILS FOR THESE DRAWINGS WERE BASED ON KNOWN DIMENSIONS AND FROM PHOTOGRAPHS. TOTAL ACCURACY CAN NOT BE GUARANTEED.

FIRE BUCKETS

NORTH ELEVATION (PARCELS OFFICE)

RETURN END OF PARCELS OFFICE UNALTERED

RENDERED PLINTH.

PART SECTION/ELEVATION
SHOWING OVERHANG OF MAIN ROOF AFTER REMOVAL OF CANOPY IN 1953

ROOF LIGHT.

USE CRAWLING BOARDS SIGN

SIGN 'GENTLEMEN'

SOUTH ELEVATION
SHOWING ORIGINAL CANOPY & ENTRANCE TO GENTS.

Station Livery

In Southern Railway days and up until the spring of 1953 the colour scheme was as follows:

Green:
> Doors and door frames; window frames and sills; corner posts; notice boards; the bottom (horizontal) board to the main cladding on the platform elevation; the cap bead and beading strips to the canopy valance; the end and bottom boards to the timber screen to the Gents'; (and possibly the exposed timber joists under – and supporting – the canopy?).

White:
> Window sashes; roof lights; edge of platform.

Cream:
> All other parts.

When repainted by BR(WR) in 1953, all areas previously green were repainted brown other than what remained of the valancing, all of which was painted cream, as indeed was the new fascia board.

MIDFORD SIGNALBOX

Midford signalbox was erected in conjunction with the doubling of the line between Midford and Wellow in 1892. The box was built to a standard design used on the 'Bath Extension', other examples of which could be seen with only detailed differences (and, of course, differing sizes to suit operating requirements) at Wellow, Midsomer Norton, Chilcompton, Binegar and Shepton Mallet. Yet a further example existed at West Pennard on the Highbridge branch.

The base of the box was constructed in limestone and housed a 16 lever locking frame. The superstructure was of timber and glazed construction on three elevations, whilst the rear wall, which incorporated the chimney stack, was part masonry and part brick built to full height. The gabled roof was slated, with decorative wooden bargeboards and finial posts, the gables infilled with vertical timber boarding. Access was by means of a straight flight of steps leading to an open verandah but alterations were made necessary to the access with the introduction of the Whitaker mechanical tablet apparatus in 1905. (Study of the relevant photographs in this publication will reveal these alterations.)

As related earlier, this original signalbox sustained severe damage when struck by trucks derailed on the single line facing points on 29th July 1936. The accompanying drawings show elevations of the flat-roofed structure provided by the Southern Railway as a 'temporary replacement' to the damaged box in August 1936, a replacement that survived until closure of the line 30 years later!

Further external changes were made as follows:-

c1952   The provision of a covered porch at the top of the access stairs. Before then the landing at the entrance to the box was 'open to the skies', the sides being clad with vertical boarding below handrail level.

1953   Change of livery from Southern Railway to BR(WR).

1958   Provision of electric light on front corner of box. The existing oil lamp fixed to the front of the box below sill level was removed.

c1962   The timber boarding/casing to the point rodding at the base of the front elevation was removed and replaced by brick infill.

The construction details of the box were as follows:

Base:
> Limestone with brick on edge sills to the 2 windows to the locking room. Flat brick arch over doorway to locking room.

Rear Wall:
> Base section in limestone. Upper section in brickwork. Chimney stack in brick with stone dressings.

Superstructure:
> Timber framed with horizontal boarding. Note the layout and differing sizes of the windows on the front elevation. (There were 5 equal-sized sashes to the front elevation of the original pre-1936 box.)

Flat Roof:
> Timber boarded with felt roofing (may have been lead underneath).

Access:
> The lower flight and quarter landing of the staircase were of brick and concrete construction. The upper flight comprised an open-tread timber staircase leading to a boarded access landing (which, as noted above, was covered in about 1952).

The livery of the box (1936 to 1953) was as follows:

Green:
> Corner posts, window framing and sills, doors, door frames, fascia boards and capping pieces, top handrails, support posts to stairs/steps, capping rail to access landing, edging strip and background to nameboard, rainwater downpipes and hopper heads, support rail for fire buckets.

White:
> Window sashes.

Cream:
> All horizontal boarding etc. to superstructure, vertical boarding to access landing, railings and staircase (excluding top handrails and support posts).

Red:
> Fire buckets (still lettered S&D.J.R.).

In 1953 those parts previously painted green were repainted in BR(WR) brown, excluding fascia boards, support posts to handrails and balcony, and rainwater pipes, all of which were included with the cream paintwork. The fire buckets were repainted but the lettering S&D.J.R. was retained.

MIDFORD SIGNALBOX
—— 1936 - 1966 ——

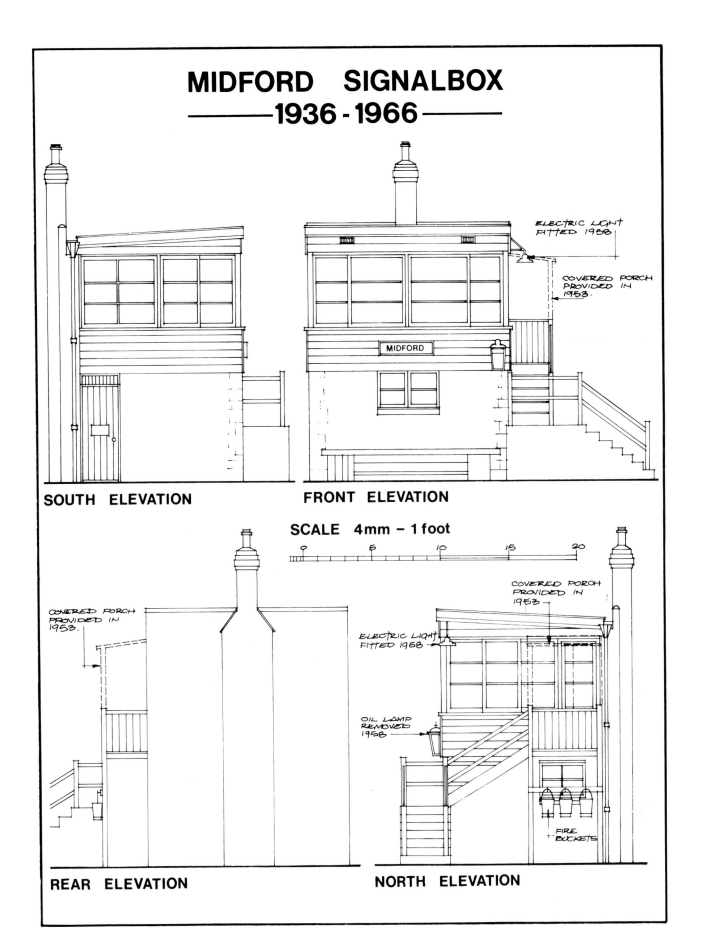

SOUTH ELEVATION

FRONT ELEVATION

ELECTRIC LIGHT
FITTED 1958

COVERED PORCH
PROVIDED IN
1953.

MIDFORD

SCALE 4mm – 1 foot

0   5   10   15   20

COVERED PORCH
PROVIDED IN
1953.

COVERED PORCH
PROVIDED IN
1953 –

ELECTRIC LIGHT
FITTED 1958 –

OIL LAMP
REMOVED
1958 –

FIRE
BUCKETS

REAR ELEVATION

NORTH ELEVATION

Stanier 'Black Five' No. 44917 and BR class 5 No. 73051 coast under Twinhoe Bridge with the 9.25 am (SO) Bournemouth-Manchester and Liverpool on 24th August 1957.   Ivo Peters

At first glance the wheelmarks made by the passage of the farmer's tractor might almost be mistaken for an overgrown single-line railway. Bridge No. 19, erected when the line to Wellow was doubled in 1892, still spans the trackbed near Lower Twinhoe Farm 20 years after close of the line.   Mac Hawkins

Two BR class 5's Nos. 73027 and 73087 have taken full advantage of the 1 in 60 descent and sweep past Ivo's parked car towards the viaduct with the 10.05 am (SO) Bournemouth-Derby on 8th July 1961, by which time the former up siding and 'Midford B' ground frame had been removed. Ivo Peters

A break in the unkempt undergrowth provides a glimpse of the former trackbed. Otherwise only the outline of Primrose Hill gives any clue to this being the same location 25 years later. Mac Hawkins

2P No. 40601 and SR Pacific No. 34042 'Dorchester' surmount the ½ mile 1 in 60 climb from Midford and swing around the curve past milepost 4½ near Lower Twinhoe with the 9.10 am (SO) Birmingham-Bournemouth on 24th August 1957.

Ivo Peters

The once well-maintained lineside cutting is now covered by the unchecked growth of a quarter of a century. A cattle feeder stands on the route of the down line. Midford Mill, long disused, still stands and can be seen to the extreme right of the scene.

Mac Hawkins

S&D 7F No. 53810 crosses Midford viaduct with an up goods train on 21st June 1955. The GW line to Camerton can be seen to the right, crossing over the Midford-Twinhoe lane which climbs Primrose Hill, passing the access gate to the up siding, south of the viaduct.   Ivo Peters

The same viewpoint in early summer 1986. Bushes and saplings sprout from the ballast whilst the lane to Twinhoe can now only be glimpsed through the trees which have grown up on the embankment south of the viaduct.   Mac Hawkins

Midford Station. This fine model was displayed at the 1986 AGM of the S&DR Trust.   M. Meadows, courtesy John Watkins

ACKNOWLEDGMENTS

I am grateful to the following for allowing me to reproduce photographs which are their copyright or are in their possession:

Ben J. Ashworth; D.W. Bartlett; David & Charles (ref. the L&GRP collection); George Dow; Colin Maggs; Ivo Peters; Peter Pike; R.C. Riley; Mrs M. Ryan; Somerset & Dorset Railway Trust Collection, courtesy Reg Randell; Col. E.A. Trotman O.B.E.; Tony Wadley; John Watkins.

In addition Mac Hawkins has supplied me with photographs taken specially for this book, including the 'now' pictures in the 'Past and Present' feature. (For readers who, like myself, are fascinated by such comparisons I commend Mac's new book *The Somerset and Dorset Then and Now*.)

I have made use of S&DJR Rule Books, Signal Notices, Appendices to Working Timetables, together with material culled from local newspapers and public record offices.

I also wish to thank and acknowledge the following people and organisations for their generous help, without which the book would have been much the poorer:

Dr Peter. E. Cattermole, who, all but single-handed, has created the superb museum of the Somerset & Dorset Railway Trust (housed at Washford station, on the West Somerset Railway, and well worth a visit); Brian Davis, for printing photographs, often at short notice; David Edgley (Wessex Newspapers) for permitting me to make use of material from the *Bath Chronicle*; C. Hale, Regional S&T Engineer, British Rail (Southern), for allowing me to reproduce official signalling plans and drawings of the installations at Midford; Duncan Harper, for use of material in his private collection; Michael Harris, editor of *Railway World* for agreeing to my request to make use of material which appeared in my own article published in November 1981; Alan Kettlety, who prepared most of the drawings and maps for me; Malcolm Lewis; Chris Osment, whose expert knowledge of all matters related to signalling on the S&D proved of great assistance; Peter J.C. Skelton, for printing the large number of negatives which Ivo allowed me to select; John Slater, editor of *The Railway Magazine*, for permission to use material from my articles previously published in that magazine; Dr. L.E. Smith, for the use of material from his collection and for the conducted tour around his delightful garden which occupies what was once a section of the old Somersetshire Coal Canal at Midford; Peter Smith (and other ex S&D personalities), for help and advice; The Somerset & Dorset Railway Trust, the Committee of which readily agreed to me using material from the Trust's bi-monthly publication, the *Bulletin*; Richard Strange (re. the Mangotsfield Railway Circle); S.G. Taylor, for the loan of Certificates awarded to him and his Midford gang (Gang 180); Chris Wake, who allowed me to read through copies of the Officers' Minute Books of the S&DJR, which he holds in his own museum, the Branston Railway Museum in Lincolnshire; Mrs. W. Wiltshire.

Finally my special thanks to Tim and Alan, my publishers, for offering me the opportunity to produce *The Somerset and Dorset at Midford* and to Sandra, my ever-suffering wife, who thought she had seen and heard the last of the S&D twenty years ago!